HEALING OF SOUL,
HEALING OF BODY

HEALING OF SOUL, HEALING OF BODY

Spiritual Leaders Unfold

the Strength & Solace

in Psalms

EDITED BY

Rabbi Simkha Y. Weintraub, CSW

A Project of the Jewish Healing Center

Jewish Lights Publishing

Woodstock, Vermont

Healing of Soul, Healing of Body:
Spiritual Leaders Unfold the Strength & Solace in Psalms

Library of Congress Cataloging-in-Publication Data
Healing of soul, healing of body : spiritual leaders unfold the strength
& solace in psalms / edited by Simkha Y. Weintraub : afterword prayer
by Sheldon Zimmerman.
p. cm.
Includes bibliographical references.
ISBN 1-879045-31-1 : $13.95
1. Jewish meditation. 2. Spiritual healing. 3. Spiritual life—Judaism.
4. Bible. O.T. Psalms—Meditations. 5. Patients—Religious life. I.
Weintraub, Simkha Y.
BM724.H397 1994   94-14798
296.7'2—dc20   CIP

10 9 8 7 6 5 4 3 2 1

Manufactured in the United States of America
Book and cover designed by Karen Savary

Published by Jewish Lights Publishing
A Division of LongHill Partners, Inc.
P.O. Box 237
Sunset Farm Offices—Route 4
Woodstock, VT 05091
Tel: (802) 457-4000 Fax: (802) 457-4004

The Jewish Healing Center gratefully acknowledges the support of Lynn Shevin Gitomer, whose generosity made possible the publication of this book.

This book is dedicated in loving memory of my grand-mother, Betty Elizabeth Gitomer (1905-1993), a woman I admired and deeply loved. Although she will not benefit from these psalms, my hopes are that you will find comfort, strength, and peace in the words that follow.

LYNN SHEVIN GITOMER
San Francisco, 1994

CONTENTS

ACKNOWLEDGMENTS

THIS IS ONE OF THOSE BOOKS FOR WHICH THE "THANK-YOUS" are endless. So many individuals and agencies have, consciously or unwittingly, contributed to its development that it is simply impossible to list them all. With apologies to those who are not named, the editor would like to express special appreciation to the following:

The deeply committed staff and board of the Jewish Healing Center for supporting this book, from inspiration through publication;

The Nathan Cummings Foundation, the Jewish Community Endowment Fund of San Francisco, the Bialis Family Foundation, the Goodman Family Foundation, and Sinai Memorial Chapel of San Francisco, for their great support of the Jewish Healing Center;

The ever-helpful staff of Jewish Lights Publishing, especially its unusually open-minded, insightful, and tolerant President and Publisher, Stuart Matlins;

The minyan-plus of contributors (and their resourceful assistants and understanding families) whose visions and voices give this book its body and soul;

The scholars and teachers of the Breslov Research Institute in Jerusalem, who amplify the redemptive words of Rabbi Nachman, worldwide;

My wife and son, parents, siblings, grandparents, aunts, uncles, and cousins, who have all helped me through illness and shared an unusually bountiful reservoir of love, patience, tolerance, concern, hope, and encouragement.

The greatest teachers, of course, are those who, in confronting illness, have joined in the search for Jewish spiritual healing. With their pain and their hope, through their questions and their affirmations, in their moments of honesty, despair, challenge, and triumph, they lighten the burden of mortality and illumine the way for all.

RABBI SIMKHA Y. WEINTRAUB, CSW
Program Consultant,
Jewish Healing Center

HOW TO USE THIS BOOK

"Turn it inside, turn it out—for all is within it..."
Pirke Avot 5:22

ON A MANHATTAN-BOUND RUSH-HOUR SUBWAY TRAIN IN Brooklyn recently, two women—one, a 30-year-old Orthodox Jew, and the other, a 55-year-old African-American—each clutched editions of the Book of Psalms and each uttered its ancient words, quietly, one in Hebrew, the other in English.

These women are on to something.

For centuries, people have turned to the Book of Psalms for solace, comfort, and catharsis, seeking guidance, meaning, hope, and reassurance—in short, spiritual healing.

This book is intended to help you—struggling with illness or helping someone who is—derive spiritual healing from Psalms.

In the late 18th century, Rabbi Nachman of Breslov (see Introduction) designated ten of the 150 entries in the Book of Psalms as "healing psalms," and we present these ten to you for your personal exploration and expression.

Acknowledging that the Biblical Psalms are somewhat alien to many people, we asked ten rabbis, spiritual leaders from the four denominational movements in American

11

Judaism, to provide some sort of bridge, some form of access, to these ancient poems of pain and praise, of humility and hope.

But How Do I Use These Psalms?

The first step is to jump in—pick a psalm and read it through, aloud if possible. Try to find a "hook," one idea or image that speaks to you or interests you in some way; once you do, try to understand what precedes that idea or image in the psalm, and what follows it. If you don't find such a hook, read the Introduction that precedes that psalm. If it still doesn't click, move on, for now at least, to another of the ten psalms.

Then What Do I Do?

Make it your own. Locate the sentence, phrase, or word that resonates loudest for you in the present moment, and try to memorize it. Consider printing it out on paper, in the size that suits your needs, and keeping it posted in an easily-spotted location. Following your personality, skills, and interests, further "acquire" your selection through chanting, meditation, movement, painting, calligraphy, creative writing, etc. You may want to make your own recording of the psalm. Make it yours in whatever way you can.

And Then?

Some more ideas:

Find partners—good friends, close relatives, trusted health care professionals, a spiritual leader or educator—and jointly explore the psalm.

Chart, on paper if possible, the movement within the psalm—its structure, shifting voices or moods, question-and-response.

Discuss and record possible interpretations of difficult passages; try to integrate (or at least tolerate) more than one understanding if none seems to fit perfectly.

Compare different translations and study traditional commentaries (see "Suggested Reading and Resources" section) together, and see which are most consonant with your own personal experience and perspective.

In time, see if you can't move through all ten psalms, arriving at a flow of meaning that derives from the themes and images of each of the ten (see the Introduction for one approach).

Consider writing your own psalm, perhaps borrowing conceptual or structural elements from these ten—or write a commentary on one of these ten, relating its message(s) to your experience with illness.

According to the followers of Rabbi Nachman, these ten psalms may be recited at any time. Rabbi Nachman recommended saying them in order without interruption.

BUT WHAT IF I CAN'T GET INTO THIS RIGHT AWAY?

"The person who says 'Amen' sincerely is counted as if the entire prayer has been said."

Shulhan Arukh, Orah Hayyim 124:1

Say "Amen," and try returning to a psalm at another juncture—another one of these ten, or one of the other 140 in the Book of Psalms (some possibilities: Psalms 3, 6, 16, 23, 27, 30, 31, 40, 69, 86, 90, 91, 116, 121, 130, and 139).

SOME THOUGHTS ON TRANSLATING PSALMS

It is universally accepted that one cannot translate great poetry and expect to achieve similar artistic impact in the second language. Poetry is neither linear nor simple, neither two-dimensional nor generic; it is not just about words but about relationships, which cannot be replicated. Elements such as cadence, rhyme, imagery, structure, and composition simply cannot be "recycled" from one culture to another, or easily transplanted from one century to the next.

Compounding this basic challenge is the fact that the

Hebrew of the Book of Psalms is, to vastly understate the situation, *problematic*—consider how frequently translations are footnoted with "meaning of Hebrew uncertain." There are numerous words, phrases, and usages that are downright obscure if not impossible to "crack," let alone render smoothly in another language.

Any reading of a psalm, like any reading of any literature, certainly of any poetic composition, must be viewed as a *midrash*—an interpretation, a commentary, a necessary but somewhat distorting re-reading of the text. This is our fate in approaching art in general, but most especially, in exploring the pages of the ancient psalms.

And yet, it is also our invitation and our delight. Because it is precisely these linguistic or cultural "gaps" that draw us in—that require us to attend to the ancient material from where we sit, to ask questions of all kinds and seek answers, even tentative ones, that will connect our tradition with our contemporary reality.

The translations here are offered, then, with a healthy dose of humility and deference to the Author of the psalms. They are meant as a bridge to the text and not as a substitute for the psalms themselves—a reflection and a refraction of the meaning to which we all aspire.

In the interests of reaching the heads and hearts of as many readers as possible, we have taken substantial liberties, including occasional shifts in gender from the Hebrew (which speaks in great measure from the male vantage point, certainly when speaking of God). Rather than replace truly difficult passages with "...", we have offered an English version that might work for some, but is certainly not the last word in re-presenting the Hebrew original. Psalm 16 was translated by Rabbi Harlan J. Wechsler; all of the other translations are by Rabbi Simkha Y. Weintraub.

We have sometimes retained the Hebrew "Adonai" in lieu of the English "God," seeking, at once, a more authentic and a more personal name for the Almighty. And where words were truly deemed multi-dimensional and thus untranslatable, we have paired the Hebrew with a partial English equivalent (such as "*Hessed*/Lovingkindness").

Our approach is motivated by the famous dictum:

"You are not required to finish the task,
but neither are you allowed to desist from it
completely."

Pirke Avot, 2:16

We know we have not finished, but trust that we have not desisted, in seeking to present these ten psalms of healing.

PUBLISHER'S NOTE:

As this book went to press, we noticed that in preparing the Hebrew text for printing, a software conversion problem shifted the *metteg* (the vertical accent mark that appears next to the vowels) in the Hebrew text. In some places, this type variance inhibits easy reading of the vocalization. We apologize for any inconvenience.

INTRODUCTION

The Ten Psalms of the Tikkun HaKlali, the Complete Remedy

If you believe that you can do damage,
then believe that you can repair!
Rabbi Nachman of Breslov,
Likutey Moharan II, 112

THE BOOK OF PSALMS IS A RICH TREASURY OF PRAYER AND reflection for many occasions and situations. Over the centuries, Jews and people of all faiths have derived comfort, guidance, reassurance, and catharsis from its 150 chapters, which reflect a wide range of experience and expression— despair and delight, horror and hope, fatigue and faith, rejection and renewal.

The Hasidic master Rabbi Nachman of Breslov (1772-1810) identified ten psalms as having special power to bring a true and complete healing: *R'fuat HaGuf* (Healing of the Body) and *R'fuat HaNefesh* (Healing of the Spirit). Rabbi Nachman designated these ten psalms the *Tikkun HaKlali*, the Complete Remedy.

WHO WAS RABBI NACHMAN OF BRESLOV?

The great-grandson of the progenitor of the Hasidic trend in Judaism, the Ba'al Shem Tov, Rabbi Nachman was a charismatic religious leader in late 18th and early 19th century Czarist Russia. In line with his influential great-grandfather and the spiritual thrust of Hasidism, Rabbi Nachman stressed the emotional, subjective, worshipful dimensions of Judaism—to complement its more cognitive, intellectual, rigorously structured aspects.

Despite his stress on joy and celebration, many have pointed to a streak of pessimism in Rabbi Nachman, who is known for his statement that "All the world is but a narrow bridge, and the essential thing is not to fear at all!" And yet, his worldview left no room for despair—he emphasized that there are many "rafts" to cling to: Faith, encouragement, melody, dance, appropriate self-criticism, communion with righteous leaders, even the very longing for a relationship with the Creator.

THE TEN KINDS OF SONG: PRAYER AS DIALOGUE

> "On the instrument of ten strings....
> ...you have made me rejoice, Adonai, in Your Work..."
>
> Psalm 92:4-5

Rabbi Nachman was particularly encouraging regarding the power of prayer. In his worldview, prayer is critical to the repair of the world, and is viewed as a dialogue between humans and their Creator. Prayer accomplishes a unique reunion, a special convergence, of people and God, of people and people, of people and the Universe.

The sages taught that the Book of Psalms is built upon ten basic kinds of song and praise:

> Rabbi Yehoshua ben Levi said: Through ten expressions of praise the Book of Psalms was composed: *Nitzuah, Niggun, Maskil, Mizmor, Shir, Ashrei, Tehillah, Tefillah, Hoda'ah,* and *Halleluyah.* Greatest of all of them is *Halleluyah,* which contains praise and the name of God in one word.
>
> *Pesahim* 117a; *Zohar* III, 101a; see also Rashi's commentary on
> Psalms 1:1

Rabbi Nachman taught that the Ten Psalms of his *Tikkun HaKlali*/Complete Remedy contain all of these ten kinds of song, and thus embody the concentrated power of the entire Book of Psalms.

Now according to the Breslov Hassidim, the followers of Rabbi Nachman, the ten kinds of song correspond to the Ten *Sefirot* of the Kabbalah, the mystical attributes through which the Creator brought the universe into being.[1] These Ten *Sefirot* are called "Direct Light," shining from the Creator to the world. Human song is viewed as a kind of "Reflected Light" in which we, God's creatures, "mirror" back the Direct Light by fulfilling God's will—through knowing God, praising God, and leading our lives in as harmonious and joyous a manner as possible.

Tradition says that the Psalms, written with *ru'ah hakodesh*, "Divine Inspiration," are most effective in mirroring back the Direct Light, bearing extra spiritual power. Indeed, they can facilitate the process of selecting good from evil, merging left with right, sweetening Judgement with supernal Mercy.[2] Through these lofty compositions, our "returning voice" is joined to the Direct One, and the Holy One Blessed Be He is reunited with the *Sh'khinah*, God's feminine aspect and in-dwelling presence.

HOW SHOULD WE RECITE THESE PSALMS?

Rabbi Nachman taught that the Psalms can have minimal value in mere recitation—one must identify with their contents in a deep and meaningful way, and seek to apply the words to oneself, to find oneself in every psalm. Towards this end, we have asked ten spiritual leaders—rabbis of different denominations, backgrounds, personalities, and ministries—to share with you their own personal "bridge" to the psalms. Some have offered introductions, others commentaries, still others deeply personal statements. All seek healing and meaning from Psalms.

Please see the section entitled "How to Use This Book" for some guidance in approaching these ten psalms.

What Is *Tikkun*?

Rabbi Nachman taught that the Covenant (in Hebrew, *b'rit*) is the foundation of the Jewish People's closeness to God. The purpose of the commandments, in his teaching, is to turn us towards, and bring us closer to, God and Godliness. And Rabbi Nachman focused not just on the technical or rote adherence to the details of this "contract" with God, but on an attitude of mind and heart, a spiritual quest for purity and devotion, a reaching for *hessed*/lovingkindness.

According to the Breslov worldview, the ultimate purpose of the Creation is to reveal God's Kingship to the world. Only when this is realized will true happiness reign. But the creation of *each and every* individual has the purpose of revealing Godliness, and a person can only be happy to the extent that s/he uncovers their innate Godliness within. As long as this revelation is incomplete, neither the individual nor the world as a whole can be completely happy.

The ultimate goal is to bring the world to a state of *tikkun*—which implies repair, correction, wholeness, perfection. *Tikkun* is both the great, cosmic goal of perfection as well as each and every individual, tiny act of reconstruction that brings about the ultimate repair. In Rabbi Nachman's teaching, the *tikkun* comes to remedy a breach in the Covenantal relationship (*p'gam ha-brit*), to bridge the separation between people and God.

The Ten Psalms as a Unit

Viewed together, the Ten Psalms reflect an unfolding of many emotions and reactions common to those dealing with illness. Although every reader should approach the Ten Psalms from his/her own individual experience and vantage point—and may thus arrive at a different understanding and personal interpretation—here is one sketch of each psalm's content, to aid in uncovering a flow of meaning and direction.

Psalm 16 starts with a powerful expression of trust and faith in God and gratitude for God's goodness. The psalmist feels the nearness of the Divine Presence and confidence in Divine protection.

Psalm 32 urges us to look deep into ourselves, to examine where and how we have distanced ourselves from God, and to return to God as the Source of true life and joy.[3]

Psalm 41 speaks explicitly about sickness, vividly portraying the torment and suffering endured by so many, expressing thanks to God for the possibility of healing, and stressing the need for caregivers to be sensitive, understanding, and supportive.

Psalm 42 beautifully depicts the yearning for God "as a hart thirsts for springs of water," describing the pain and suffering of both the individual and the nation in exile while affirming the hope of ultimate deliverance.

Psalm 59 is a cry from the heart for God to deliver us from the forces that oppress us and cast us down, echoing David's plea for rescue from Saul's soldiers and his thanksgiving upon receiving Divine refuge and support.

Psalm 77 is an important turning point in this collection, beginning with an expression of anguish and abandonment, the pain and persecution of a long, bitter exile—but moving into an affirmation of faith that God is ever-present and compassionate, despite appearances to the contrary.

Psalm 90 offers a profound comment on human destiny, contrasting human frailty and the brevity of human life with God's eternity and omnipotence, asking God for wisdom, joy, security, support, and compassion.

Psalm 105, after calls to sing and praise, traces the national history of the Jewish People from the covenant with the Patriarchs and Matriarchs through the Exodus from Egypt, which serves as a prototype of Redemption.

Psalm 137 takes us back to the acute pain of exile, weaving in nine verses a tapestry of grief, despair, memory, affirmation, and anger...which may be viewed as the proverbial darkness that comes before the light, as these Ten Psalms conclude with Psalm 150, a paean and musical symphony of praises.

OTHER PRACTICES TO FURTHER *TIKKUN*

In addition to the Ten Psalms, there are several concrete, specific practices that Rabbi Nachman and the Breslov Hassidim recommend as part of the *Tikkun HaKlali*:

TZ'DAKAH: ELEVATING THE MATERIAL AS PART OF TIKKUN

"Great is *Tz'dakah*, for it brings the Redemption nearer..."

Sefer HaMidot, Rabbi Nachman's classic collection of aphorisms, first published in Mogolov, 1811, *Tz'dakah*, 2-7

Tz'dakah—which literally means "justice" but which has come to designate what is known as "charity" or "philanthropy" in English—is a critical element in "eradicating the wedge" and repairing the chasm between the material and spiritual dimensions of life. *Tz'dakah* represents, in fact, the rededication of the former dimension to the latter, the proper realignment of priorities. The Jewish tradition demands *tz'dakah* even from the poor person, because the issue is not only one of the bottom line but of relating to the world through justice, concern, and active involvement.

Extending this concept, one realizes that even—especially?—those who are ill can reach out to those in need with empathic concern and an acute sense of justice. Many who are suffering or who have survived serious illness have discovered how potent they can be in repairing the world around them—as volunteer service providers in shelters or hunger projects, as fundraisers for all kinds of "*tz'dakahs*" (medical research, political advocacy, academic institution building, environmental projects, intergroup relations, and on and on), even in assisting someone down the hall in the medical center. At the same time, this brings new meaning and new life to their existence, and concretely builds a better society and a better world. "Down," perhaps—but not "out." Tangible *tikkun*.

The *Mikvah*: Immersion and *Tikkun*

Rabbi Nachman taught that the first stage of the remedy is immersion in a *mikvah*, the Jewish ritual bath. With its powerful connotations of re-emergence and re-dedication, the *mikvah* facilitates a process of both "return" and "renewal," of growth and change—as well as getting back to basics, becoming one with nature, "going with the flow."

For those for whom going to the *mikvah* is alien, impossible, or forbidding, one might consider a simple ritual hand-washing before saying psalms. Take a cup of cool water and ritually pour it, first over the right hand and then over the left, and then recite the following verse (Psalms 26:6): "I wash my hands in cleanliness; and I will encircle Your altar, O God."[4] Psalm 23, which speaks of "tranquil waters" and how "my cup overflows," is an appropriate addition as well, to this simple but rich ritual of emergence and regeneration.

Some people utilize these water rituals to mark personally significant transitions or changes in status—for example, at the conclusion of treatments or on the anniversary of a difficult diagnosis or surgery.

Invoking the *Tzaddikim* for *Tikkun*

"Mentioning the names of the *Tzaddikim* has the power to bring about a change in the Creation and alter Nature..."

Sefer HaMidot, Tzaddik, B, 20

"The *Tzaddikim* are even greater after death than in their lifetime..."

Talmud, *Hullin* 7b

In the Breslov tradition, the *Tzaddik*, "the Righteous One," is the most perfect exemplar of the Covenant. The *Tzaddik* is, indeed, a very unusual, maybe even ideal, individual—someone who is solely motivated by his or her good *yetser* (inclination), who has banished material desires from his or her heart, who has not only subjugated

evil but driven it out entirely, leaving only goodness within (*Likutey Moharan* I, 8:5 and I, 49:1).

And yet, we know that the *Tzaddik* is defined as "one
whose merits outweigh his sins" (Maimonides, 12th century, *Mishneh Torah, Hilkhot T'shuvah* 3:1)—i.e., the attainment
of this status depends not on some inherited constitution,
innate qualities, or intrinsic superiority, but on *deeds*. You
are what you do. Thus, Rabbi Nachman taught that "Every
man can attain the highest level. It depends on nothing but
your own free choice" (see *Rabbi Nahman's Wisdom*, "His
Praises," #26). The spirituality of the *Tzaddik* is at once a
very lofty, elevated level of sanctity—but one rooted in the
very real, here-and-now letter *and* spirit of the Torah.

"The soul of a creature is its name," says the Book of
Genesis (2:19). Names embody the very specific and potent
essence of an individual; through its name, which contains
its form and nature, every creature derives vitality. This
explains why, to the Breslov Hassidim, it is such a great
and powerful thing to mention the names of the
Tzaddikim—summoning, as it were, their righteousness,
good deeds, noble qualities, special accomplishments...the
particular "Torah" of their souls and spirits. Mentioning
the name of *Tzaddik*, one can draw on their holiness and
reach for their merit and purity on one's own journey of
return to God.

Finally, according to the Breslovers, going to the grave-
sides of *Tzaddikim* to pray helps even more than merely
invoking their names, since the sanctity of their burial
place is seen as a *tikkun* for the Covenant (see *Likutey
Moharan*, 11, 109). In this tradition, in going to the grave of
a *Tzaddik* one can, through heartfelt prayer and the yearning to return to God, become encompassed in the soul of
the *Tzaddik*, and thereby in the Infinity of God.

In point of fact, the practice of visiting the graves of
Tzaddikim is an ancient one—Jews did so in times of personal and national distress, seeking mercy, deliverance,
and forgiveness. Although this may seem morbid or
depressing to some, for many, visiting graves (of relatives,

friends, or of accomplished individuals) is an experience of affirmation, of connecting to the chain of life, of drawing on the strength of those who have passed on. Recalling the best qualities and highest achievements of others can be ennobling and inspiring. Memory can heal.

SHALOM/WHOLENESS

Said the Holy One, Blessed be God:

> "There is no affliction
> for which there does not exist a cure;
> the therapy and medicament for every affliction is
> discernible.
> If you seek that misfortune befall not your body,
> engage in the study of Torah,
> for it is a therapy for the entire body."
> —*Midrash Tanhuma*, Yitro, 8

We wish it were possible to promise that this *tikkun* would cure cancer, reverse AIDS, or even heal broken bones. This we cannot do. But the contributors and sponsors of this book join in urging you, the reader, to turn to the Jewish tradition and to the Jewish community and seek healing of the spirit. There is much to be mined. We pray and believe that your outstretched arm will not remain empty or cold, and that your cry will be heard and answered.

To you, to all—*shalom*/wholeness.

RABBI SIMKHA Y. WEINTRAUB, CSW
Program Consultant, Jewish Healing Center

CONTINUALLY BEFORE ME

Commentary on Psalm 16

Rabbi Harlan J. Wechsler

THE PSALMIST IS ILL, ALONE, WANTING TO HOPE AND YET NEED-
ing reassurance that hope is worth the effort. Picture with
me the psalmist's life experience as captured by his words.

David needs protection, so he opens by asking God to
be there for him (v. 1). He then speaks to himself, as we all
do; he addresses a part of himself as if he were another person (v. 2). In truth, we are many persons. One side of
David, in particular, needs to be addressed: The side which
feels unworthy. There is something intimidating about his
position: Having to call on God without really having prepared for that call. Isn't it odd to be turning now to God,
now that we are in the foxhole in need of God's help? It is
embarrassing even to begin — but if not now, when?

This sense of inadequacy, distance, or unworthiness
persists (v. 3). There are many in league with God, friends
who have ready entree. Yes, it makes sense for *them* to turn
to God, and it makes sense for God to turn to them. But
here am I; does it make sense for *me*?

Indeed, those who are at home with God seem to have
a regimen for pain management. They can turn beyond

א מִכְתָּם לְדָוִד, שָׁמְרֵנִי אֵל כִּי־חָסִיתִי בָךְ.

ב אָמַרְתְּ לַיהוה, אֲדֹנָי אָתָּה, טוֹבָתִי בַּל־עָלֶיךָ.

ג לִקְדוֹשִׁים אֲשֶׁר־בָּאָרֶץ הֵמָּה, וְאַדִּירֵי כָּל־חֶפְצִי־בָם.

ד יִרְבּוּ עַצְּבוֹתָם אַחֵר מָהָרוּ;

בַּל־אַסִּיךְ נִסְכֵּיהֶם מִדָּם,

וּבַל־אֶשָּׂא אֶת־שְׁמוֹתָם עַל־שְׂפָתָי.

ה יהוה מְנָת־חֶלְקִי וְכוֹסִי, אַתָּה תּוֹמִיךְ גּוֹרָלִי.

---

themselves. But David feels he cannot (v. 4). He is in need
of God, and he is burdened by his own guilt, by his own
inadequacy. Perhaps he feels that he is suffering because he
deserves it. Or perhaps suffering can come to anyone, but
he is afraid that you have to deserve God's special atten-
tion before you can have the temerity to say: "Heal me!"

Soon, though, the doubting introduction gives way to
David's other side, the side that knows the Lord cares for
him (v. 5). Not even our humility or our doubt can convince
us that God is not there for us when we need God. To the
contrary: The destiny of each of us is tied to the Lord and
the Lord's concern.

PSALM 16

1. *These are among David's golden words:*
   Watch over me, God,
       for I seek refuge in You.
2. You said to the Lord:
       "You are my Master,
           but my good fortune is not Your concern.
3. "Rather, the holy ones on the earth
           —You care for them
               and for the great ones whom I should
                   emulate.
4. "When their pain multiplies,
         they know to speedily turn to another.
       But I cannot even pour their libations because of
                 guilt,
       I cannot even lift their names to my lips."
5. The Lord is the Portion, which is mine by right,
         my Cup.
         You nurture my destiny.

This shift, however tentative it may be, opens the psalmist up to the realization that pain and suffering have multiple messages. There are some pains, like that of giving birth, which yield gifts as yet unknown (v. 6). How do we know what life has in store? How do we know what significance tomorrow will bring? Like a newborn baby, our lives may soon begin again.

To the extent that I have control over my thoughts, let me picture them this way: As a new and beautiful beginning. There are limited ways to respond to pain. Like a scratch in a precious jewel, I might be tempted to see it as my ruination. But I can also try to artistically create a rose

חֲבָלִים נָפְלוּ-לִי בַּנְּעִמִים, אַף-נַחֲלָת שָׁפְרָה עָלָי. ו

אֲבָרֵךְ אֶת-יְהוה אֲשֶׁר יְעָצָנִי, ז
אַף-לֵילוֹת יִסְּרוּנִי כִלְיוֹתָי.

שִׁוִּיתִי יהוה לְנֶגְדִּי תָמִיד, כִּי מִימִינִי בַּל-אֶמּוֹט. ח

לָכֵן שָׂמַח לִבִּי וַיָּגֶל כְּבוֹדִי, אַף-בְּשָׂרִי יִשְׁכֹּן לָבֶטַח. ט

כִּי לֹא-תַעֲזֹב נַפְשִׁי לִשְׁאוֹל, י
לֹא-תִתֵּן חֲסִידְךָ לִרְאוֹת שָׁחַת.

תּוֹדִיעֵנִי אֹרַח חַיִּים, יא
שֹׂבַע שְׂמָחוֹת אֶת-פָּנֶיךָ,
נְעִמוֹת בִּימִינְךָ נֶצַח.

from it which will make the jewel more valuable, more mine, invested with the totality of my life, the unique wholeness which is my inheritance.

With this realignment, the possibility of a new direction, David blesses the Lord (v. 7). From deep down in his being, he knows that the conflicts of conscience, the feelings of worthlessness which afflict him from time to time, do not tell the whole story. And God does not want him to wallow in his sorrow. But rather it is a lofty, a pristine, and a powerful feeling to know deep inside that I am so close to God, so near to the Lord's purpose, God's power, and the beauty of my life which is the way God sees me, that I

6. Labor pains turn into pleasantness—
        so, too, I must see my inheritance of beauty.
7. I will bless the Lord who counsels me,
        though at night my conscience afflicts me.
8. I keep the Lord continually before me;
        because of God-Who-is-my-Right-Hand,
        I shall not break down.
9. So my mind is happy,
        my whole being joyful;
            even my body rests secure.
10. For You shall not abandon my soul
        to the world of the dead,
            nor let the one who loves You
                see his own grave.
11. Give me directions on life's road.
        With Your Presence,
            I am filled up with joys,
                with the delights that ever come
                    from Your Strong Arm.

can do that which is best: bless the Lord. I might have felt bereft and without the ability to bless. I might have found myself more tempted to curse. But feeling God near, I am able to bless, even now in my pain.

Not only that. I shall keep the Lord always before me (v. 8). My mind focuses on many things, my eyes look in many directions. And the result, at this moment, is the creation of difficulties. Because what I need is a clear sense of God, I will use my consciousness to remind myself of the Lord time and again.

What a payoff there is, too. The Lord is just the strength I need, the support for my flagging energy, both spiritual and physical. Indeed, once I have that, I shall be able to cope. And for me, coping means a great deal. It means not crumbling under the weight of the pain I bear.

Then my soul rests. There is a glorious joy that I feel seeping into me, into my mind, and, even deeper, into my being (v. 9). That point in me which is my center was, for some while, unclear. And now, the joyfulness that I feel spills over into my body. My body is what needs so much help, and my body is helped by God because my joyful soul gives it the energy it has lacked. Just what I need.

The psalmist—and I, the reader—can reaffirm that it is not death but life that God calls into being (v. 10). I am so afraid of death, so afraid that were God to leave me alone, were my body to have to operate on its own, solely subject to its physical laws and those who know how to minister to it from a solely scientific perspective, then it might give out. But it won't because God adds that extra bit of life and of strength. After all this mental and physical agony, it is good to know that I am not over, but starting anew.

A prayer (v. 11): I have not come to the end of my road, but I am now on one of life's byways. Oh to learn from every turn taken! But even better, to get insight from the Lord.

How good it is to be secure, to have a refuge from all that is assailing me. The Lord is that refuge. His presence is so precious. I am weak and the Lord is strong. And God's strength is in my service. Now I am revived, human, myself. Ready.

AFRAID BUT NOT ALONE

Meditation on Psalm 32

Rabbi Irving Greenberg

THIS IS A PSALM OF THANKSGIVING FOR RECOVERY FROM sickness.

At the start, the patient is in total isolation, trapped in illness, sunk in him/herself, wasting away. Alone, oppressed by sin but not daring to speak its name, the psalmist watches helplessly as the unforgiving guilt implacably consumes the inner reserves of vigor—body and soul. Then, in a desperate bid to break out of the strangling grip of death, the patient determines to confess the sin.

It is also possible that when bad things happen to good people, good people are all too quick to blame themselves. They assume that God wants to punish them. If this is our case, it does not change the facts. It only means that this innocent person threw him/herself on the mercy of Adonai (Loving God; v. 5).

The confession was the turning point. Once the patient put the sin—and the possibility of dying—out in the open, then the deepest truth was revealed. No sin is so great as to exhaust God's infinite love and forgiveness. Now, facing God directly—focused on the Loving Presence and not only on the finite, presumed guilt—the person discovers a

א לְדָוִד מַשְׂכִּיל;

אַשְׁרֵי נְשׂוּי־פֶּשַׁע, כְּסוּי חֲטָאָה.

ב אַשְׁרֵי־אָדָם לֹא יַחְשֹׁב יהוה לוֹ עָוֹן,

וְאֵין בְּרוּחוֹ רְמִיָּה.

ג כִּי־הֶחֱרַשְׁתִּי בָּלוּ עֲצָמָי, בְּשַׁאֲגָתִי כָּל־הַיּוֹם.

ד כִּי יוֹמָם וָלַיְלָה תִּכְבַּד עָלַי יָדֶךָ,

נֶהְפַּךְ לְשַׁדִּי בְּחַרְבֹנֵי קַיִץ סֶלָה.

ה חַטָּאתִי אוֹדִיעֲךָ, וַעֲוֹנִי לֹא־כִסִּיתִי,

אָמַרְתִּי, אוֹדֶה עֲלֵי פְשָׁעַי לַיהוה;

וְאַתָּה נָשָׂאתָ עֲוֹן חַטָּאתִי סֶלָה.

ו עַל־זֹאת יִתְפַּלֵּל כָּל־חָסִיד אֵלֶיךָ לְעֵת מְצֹא,

healing release. Reminded that God is always on the side of life because God is the One who desires life, the sick person feels a flood of emotions: Hope, trust, anticipation, joy. The words tumble out: "You are my Shelter; You protect me from distress, from enemies; You surround me with the joy of deliverance!" (v. 7).

In this case, the cure soon followed. Now the patient is able to look beyond the wall of anxiety and fear which has surrounded the sickbed. Silence turns into dialogue. God speaks: "I will teach you Wisdom; I will illumine the path you must take; My eye will advise you and guide you" (v. 8).

Joyfully carried away by the surge of wholeness and

PSALM 32

1. *A Song of David, of instruction:*
   Happy is one whose sins are forgiven,
       whose transgressions are wiped away.
2. Happy is one whose wrongdoing Adonai passes over,
       whose Spirit is without deceit.
3. When I kept silent, my bones wore out;
       I groaned all day in fear.
4. Day and night Your Hand weighed heavily upon me;
       My marrow turned dry, parched as by the heat of
                       Summer,
           Selah.
5. So now, I will acknowledge transgression,
       I will no longer obscure wrongdoing;
           Even as I began to say, 'I admit my sins before
                                   Adonai,'
           You forgave my errors and misdeeds, *Selah.*
6. Let one devoted to You offer this prayer
       at those moments when You may be found:
           'When trials and troubles come,
           may they not flood in a deluge of destruction!'

restoration, the patient calls out to all who would listen. "Many are the troubles of the wicked, but one who trusts in Adonai will be enveloped by *Hessed*/Lovingkindness" (v. 10). Jubilantly the restored person cries out: "Rejoice in Adonai! Exult, righteous ones! Shout for joy, all who are upright in heart!" (v. 11).

Is this, then, a psalm only for those who are cured? Perhaps unrestrained joy can only come from one who has been healed. But the deepest truth of the experience may yet be available to totally innocent persons who are sick due to no fault of their own. It may even be available to one who is not cured yet; even to one who will not be cured.

רַק לְשֵׁטֶף מַיִם רַבִּים אֵלָיו לֹא יַגִּיעוּ.

אַתָּה סֵתֶר לִי, מִצַּר תִּצְּרֵנִי;
רָנֵּי פַלֵּט תְּסוֹבְבֵנִי סֶלָה.

אַשְׂכִּילְךָ וְאוֹרְךָ בְּדֶרֶךְ־זוּ תֵלֵךְ, אִיעֲצָה עָלֶיךָ עֵינִי.

אַל־תִּהְיוּ כְּסוּס כְּפֶרֶד אֵין הָבִין;
בְּמֶתֶג־וָרֶסֶן עֶדְיוֹ לִבְלוֹם, בַּל קְרֹב אֵלֶיךָ.

רַבִּים מַכְאוֹבִים לָרָשָׁע,
וְהַבּוֹטֵחַ בַּיהוה חֶסֶד יְסוֹבְבֶנּוּ.

שִׂמְחוּ בַיהוה וְגִילוּ צַדִּיקִים,
וְהַרְנִינוּ כָּל־יִשְׁרֵי־לֵב.

The truth is: When you are sinking, when you are totally wrapped in your own fear and pain, it is still possible to
break out. God's Loving Presence surrounds you at all
times; God shares your pain as only an infinite consciousness can. *Hashem** feels your hurt, kisses your wound com-
passionately. The divine steadfast love enfolds you even
when the longed-for miracle does not come.

Pain can obscure but it cannot degrade your precious-
ness to *Hashem*; fear can erode but not cancel the truth of

---

*Hashem, literally "The Name," is a respectful alternative to *Adonai*,
the appellative used often in prayer. It can also be somewhat more
familiar, personal, even intimate.

7. You are my Shelter,
      You protect me from distress, from enemies,
            You surround me with the joy of deliverance,
                  Selah.
8. (You have said:)
      'I will teach you Wisdom,
        I will illumine the path you must take,
        My eye will advise you and guide you.'
9.   Do not be like a horse or a mule who cannot
                        understand,
            who, with a bit and a bridle,
            must be restrained during grooming,
            so that they do not come too close and attack.
10. Many are the troubles of the wicked,
      but one who trusts in Adonai
            will be enveloped by *Hessed*/Lovingkindness.
11. Rejoice in Adonai!
      Exult, righteous ones!
        Shout for joy, all who are upright in heart!

your being beloved. You are an image of God, of infinite worth, unique, irreplaceable. God's face is toward you, God's eye is on you at all times. If you can bring yourself to look, to sense the divine tears of love and sympathy, you will know that you are one but you are not alone. You will be healed; even if not, you will be loved.

With this truth fixed firmly in your soul, you may yet sing out joyfully the song of existence embraced. But even if not rescued, the one who trusts in a Loving God is surrounded by steadfast love. Listen. The voice speaks. "Fear not, for I am with you."

FROM ANGER AND ANGUISH TO HEALING AND WHOLENESS

Introduction to Psalm 41

Rabbi Rachel Cowan

AS WE STRUGGLE TO COME TO TERMS WITH ILLNESS, WE HEAR our own voices in this meditation on suffering. The soul-wrestling of the psalmist speaks powerfully to us. Overwhelmed by the rush of fear, anger, and grief, she wonders where will she find the strength and courage to face her situation. Empathizing with her anguish, we nonetheless see that she has only begun the long journey to comprehend her situation and to transcend it. Right now, the faith she asserts so bravely at the end is hollow. She is alone. Many of us know that pain.

Lying in bed after the diagnosis, confused by the bewildering choices of treatments, weak and exhausted, she asks herself the inevitable question, "Why *me*?" She was one who always (v. 2) "attends to the needy," and, in general, she was (v. 3) "considered fortunate on this earth."

She is her own first target (v. 5): "Adonai, have pity / Heal my soul, for I have sinned against you!" She must deserve this illness, for why else would she be punished? Reviewing her life over these past few years, she finds so

א לַמְנַצֵּחַ מִזְמוֹר לְדָוִד.

ב אַשְׁרֵי מַשְׂכִּיל אֶל־דָּל, בְּיוֹם רָעָה יְמַלְּטֵהוּ יהוה.

ג יהוה יִשְׁמְרֵהוּ וִיחַיֵּהוּ, וְאֻשַּׁר בָּאָרֶץ,
וְאַל־תִּתְּנֵהוּ בְּנֶפֶשׁ אֹיְבָיו.

ד יהוה יִסְעָדֶנּוּ עַל־עֶרֶשׂ דְּוָי,
כָּל־מִשְׁכָּבוֹ הָפַכְתָּ בְחָלְיוֹ.

ה אֲנִי־אָמַרְתִּי יהוה חָנֵּנִי, רְפָאָה נַפְשִׁי,
כִּי־חָטָאתִי לָךְ.

ו אוֹיְבַי יֹאמְרוּ רַע לִי, מָתַי יָמוּת וְאָבַד שְׁמוֹ.

ז וְאִם־בָּא לִרְאוֹת שָׁוְא יְדַבֵּר, לִבּוֹ יִקְבָּץ־אָוֶן לוֹ;
יֵצֵא לַחוּץ יְדַבֵּר.

---

many flaws. She did not visit her father enough when he was ill, she screams at her children too often, she got the job her colleague had desperately wanted. She is often stressed, she is too fat, she eats the wrong foods, she doesn't exercise. Maybe she had wanted this. Her psyche colluded with her biology to transform some cell, or to fail to fight some cell, and now she is ill. Somehow, she feels, she deserves this.

There is even some comfort in blaming herself, for it helps her feel she has some control over the situation—the power to change our behavior. If, however, she can be gentle with herself, she may find in illness an opportunity for

Psalm 41

1. *To the Chief Musician: A Song of David*
2. Happy is one who attends to the needy;
    On an evil day, Adonai will rescue her.
3. Adonai will guard her, Adonai will give her life;
    She will be considered fortunate on this earth,
        not subject to the whims of enemies.
4. Adonai will nurture her on her sickbed;
    Even when her illness advances, and her rest is
        disturbed,
    You will attend to her and turn things around.
5. As for me, I said,
    'Adonai, have pity;
    Heal my soul, for I have sinned against You.'
6. My enemies speak evil against me:
    'When will she die and her name be obliterated?'
7. Even when my enemy comes to visit me,
    her concern is empty and false;
    her heart gathers malicious thoughts,
        which she then goes out and spreads.

---

t'shuvah, for turning her life in a direction that is more clearly aligned with her true values.

Illness does not cause her faith to break. She has not yet begun, though, to reshape it in face of her experience. She has not wrestled with God. Rather, she casts God as avenger, not as healer. She prays that God will become an ally to destroy her enemies, who, alas, include her friends. "Punish them, and I will know You are just, that there is fairness in the world." *They* should be suffering, not her— they who speak falsely when they visit, who gossip afterward, who predict a poor prognosis. Even her best friend has been disloyal. Nobody really understands her, nobody

ח יַחַד עָלַי יִתְלַחֲשׁוּ כָּל־שֹׂנְאָי, עָלַי יַחְשְׁבוּ רָעָה לִי.

ט דְּבַר־בְּלִיַּעַל יָצוּק בּוֹ, וַאֲשֶׁר שָׁכַב לֹא־יוֹסִיף לָקוּם.

י גַּם־אִישׁ שְׁלוֹמִי אֲשֶׁר־בָּטַחְתִּי בוֹ, אוֹכֵל לַחְמִי,
הִגְדִּיל עָלַי עָקֵב.

יא וְאַתָּה יְהוָה חָנֵּנִי וַהֲקִימֵנִי, וַאֲשַׁלְּמָה לָהֶם.

יב בְּזֹאת יָדַעְתִּי כִּי־חָפַצְתָּ בִּי, כִּי לֹא־יָרִיעַ אֹיְבִי עָלָי.

יג וַאֲנִי בְּתֻמִּי תָּמַכְתָּ בִּי, וַתַּצִּיבֵנִי לְפָנֶיךָ לְעוֹלָם.

יד בָּרוּךְ יְהוָה אֱלֹהֵי יִשְׂרָאֵל
מֵהָעוֹלָם וְעַד־הָעוֹלָם,
אָמֵן וְאָמֵן.

---

really cares. She is alone, weak, hurting. They are well. They live in a different place from the one to which she has been unwillingly transported. They live in the land of the well. She in the land of the sick.

She is in a place many of us can recognize. But it is not a place we can afford to stay for long, once we have vented our anger, plumbed the depths of betrayal and isolation. For she has cut herself off from her most important source of strength—her community—and she is seeking from God a false solace.

To begin to find healing, she will need to reach out to others, and to let others reach out to her. Starting with one

8. Together, they whisper against me, all my enemies,
   they plot evil against me, they explain my suffering
   away.
9. 'All her evil has returned to haunt her through this
   illness,'
   they say,
   'And now that she has succumbed,
   she will never get up again.'
10. Even my intimate friend,
    whom I trusted, who ate my bread,
    has turned on me, has ambushed me!
11. But You, Adonai,
    Take pity on me,
    Be gracious to me,
    Lift me up and I shall repay them.
12. By Your Healing I will know that You accept me,
    that my enemy does not shout triumphantly over
    me.
13. You will support me because of my integrity,
    You will let me abide in Your presence forever.
14. Blessed is Adonai, God of Israel,
    from eternity to eternity—
    Amen and Amen!

or two friends, she can begin to let people see her when she is ill and wan and not at her best. They can help her reestablish a relationship with her best friend. Perhaps for now she is not strong enough for honest discussion, but if she asks for help—a phone call, a meal, a visit—the two of them could realize their importance to each other.

Through connections with family and friends, she can begin to emerge from her depression. She can begin to reaffirm her own worthiness. She knows she has been well thought of, and that she has a gift for empathy. Now, knowing pain and despair, she will be able to reach out with empathy to others.

So many of us, when we become ill, do as the psalmist did. We begrudge others their health, and lose them as allies in regaining our health. We are too proud to ask for support. Our prayers reflect the despair of this psalm. But our prayers often contain the wisdom that can lead to our healing as well, just as this psalm does. Our healing does not lie in self-pity or fantasies of revenge. It is in touching the deepest part of ourselves (and we all have wells that run very deep), in seeking comfort from God, and in reaching out to friends. Allowing ourselves to be comforted, we can comfort others, and bring about great *tikkun*/repair to our world.

This process may take a while. Nothing is easy when we are ill. But it can happen gradually. Then our prayers will change from calls for vengeance to cries to the One-Who-Heals-the-Shattered-Heart to help our heart to heal.

And as we learn to find comfort from a healing God, we will truly mean it when we say (vv. 13-14):

"You will support me because of my integrity,
      You will let me abide in your presence forever.
Blessed is Adonai, God of Israel,
from eternity to eternity—
      Amen and Amen!"

THE REMARKABLE FAITH OF A DOWNCAST SOUL

Introduction to Psalm 42

Rabbi Charles Sheer

IT WAS PROBABLY THIRTY YEARS AGO WHEN I FIRST HEARD Rav Joseph B. Soloveitchik expound on the opening phrase of Psalm 42: "Like a hind crying for springs of water, so my soul cries out for You, O God; my soul thirsts for God, for the living *El*/Almighty." A nature-lover since my youth, I was immediately drawn to the lovely opening metaphor of the hind. I conjured up an image of a spindly-legged Bambi driven by thirst to approach the waterhole. In my imagination, the vulnerable, delicate creature twitched her ears nervously, glancing about to assure that no predator was stalking nearby. While I was appreciating the artful nature of the opening metaphor, the Rav spoke passionately about the psalmist who longs, with much religious thirst, for the Almighty. "My soul thirsts for God" was, according to Rav Soloveitchik, the refrain of the lonely man of faith who desires to reach the state of intense God-consciousness.

Listening to the eloquent and profound insights of my teacher, I realized, with some sadness and disappointment, that I could not honestly declare that my soul really

מב

א לַמְנַצֵּחַ מַשְׂכִּיל לִבְנֵי־קֹרַח.

ב כְּאַיָּל תַּעֲרֹג עַל־אֲפִיקֵי־מָיִם,
כֵּן נַפְשִׁי תַעֲרֹג אֵלֶיךָ אֱלֹהִים.

ג צָמְאָה נַפְשִׁי לֵאלֹהִים, לְאֵל חָי;
מָתַי אָבוֹא וְאֵרָאֶה פְּנֵי אֱלֹהִים.

ד הָיְתָה־לִּי דִמְעָתִי לֶחֶם יוֹמָם וָלָיְלָה,
בֶּאֱמֹר אֵלַי כָּל־הַיּוֹם אַיֵּה אֱלֹהֶיךָ.

ה אֵלֶּה אֶזְכְּרָה וְאֶשְׁפְּכָה עָלַי נַפְשִׁי,
כִּי אֶעֱבֹר בַּסָּךְ, אֶדַּדֵּם עַד־בֵּית אֱלֹהִים;
בְּקוֹל־רִנָּה וְתוֹדָה הָמוֹן חוֹגֵג.

"thirsted" for God. Although I was on the way to the water-source and had experienced some wonderful moments of inspiration, my religious quest was not as innocent or focused as that of the driven hind of our psalm. And since that time my faith journey has involved digressions and pauses, especially during the period when I suffered through the illness and loss of a loved one.

If the opening words of Psalm 42 portray the quest of a deeply devout person, as my teacher interpreted, I am convinced that this is no expression of a static faith. The author immediately records that he is now in a very different place vis-a-vis God. In the following line the author speaks of a sense of abandonment and estrangement as he laments:

PSALM 42

1. *To the Chief Musician; Instruction to the Sons of Korah*
2. Like a hind crying for springs of water,
    so my soul cries out for You, O God.
3. My soul thirsts for God,
        for the living *El*/Almighty;
        O, when will I come to appear before God?
4. My tears have been my food,
        day and night;
            my enemies taunt me all day, asking,
            'Where is your God?'
5. This I remember, and pour out my soul within me—
        how I used to walk with the crowd,
        moving with them, the festive throng, up to the
        House of God,*
            with joyous shouts of praise to God
                a multitude celebrating the festival!

"O, when will I come to appear before God!" (v. 3).

The psalmist initially states that this feeling of distance from God is the result of his *physical* exile from the land. "In the land of the Jordan River and Mount Hermon's peaks" (v. 7) he recollects joyous pilgrimage celebrations when he "walked with the crowd, moving with them, the festive throng, up to the House of God, with joyous shouts of praise" (v. 5). Now he can only treasure the memory of his spiritual journeys to and within the Temple and his awareness of God's "proximity" to him and His people.

*The reference is to the festival pilgrimages to the ancient Temple in Jerusalem

מַה־תִּשְׁתּוֹחֲחִי נַפְשִׁי, וַתֶּהֱמִי עָלָי; ,

הוֹחִלִי לֵאלֹהִים, כִּי־עוֹד אוֹדֶנּוּ יְשׁוּעוֹת פָּנָיו.

אֱלֹהַי, עָלַי נַפְשִׁי תִשְׁתּוֹחָח, ,

עַל־כֵּן אֶזְכָּרְךָ מֵאֶרֶץ יַרְדֵּן וְחֶרְמוֹנִים, מֵהַר מִצְעָר.

תְּהוֹם־אֶל־תְּהוֹם קוֹרֵא לְקוֹל צִנּוֹרֶיךָ, ,

כָּל־מִשְׁבָּרֶיךָ וְגַלֶּיךָ עָלַי עָבָרוּ.

יוֹמָם יְצַוֶּה יְהוה חַסְדּוֹ, וּבַלַּיְלָה שִׁירֹה עִמִּי; ,

תְּפִלָּה לְאֵל חַיָּי.

Upon reflection it becomes apparent that the psalmist is expressing not a physical but an *existential* exile. His feeling of abandonment is derived from his interior feeling and psyche, not his location. The psalmist's description of himself paints a melancholy picture. "My tears have been my food, day and night; my enemies taunt me all day, asking, 'Where is your God?'" (v. 4). This is the anguish of a truly religious person whose course is strewn with detours.

Anyone who has been through great suffering or loss can understand these images. In the midst of our pain, life seems as fragile as the hind. We feel utterly abandoned by God. As we confront our illness or adversity, we lose our hope and our appetite for food and drink. The rabbis, in a

6. Why so downcast, my soul?
   Why disquieted within me?
       Have hope in God!
           For I will yet praise Him
           for deliverance, for His presence.
7. My God, my soul is cast down within me;
       as I remember You in the land of the Jordan River,
           and Mount Hermon's peaks,
               and the smaller mountain of Sinai.
8. Deep cries out to deep,
       the sounds of the opened sluices of heaven;
           all Your breakers and Your billows
           have swept over me.
9. By day, Adonai will command His *Hessed*/Loving-
                                        kindness,
       and at night, His resting place will be with me;
           This is my prayer to the Almighty, God of my
                                        life.

midrash to our psalm, expressed it so precisely: "From here you learn that distress satiates man and that he doesn't need to eat...and from here (you learn that) crying satiates, hence it says, 'tears have been my food...'" (*Midrash Shohar Tov*).

In the next lines (vv. 8-12), as the psalmist bares more of his tormented soul, he continues to use water as the organizing metaphor. Whereas earlier water was depicted as a nourishing agent, it now becomes a terrifying and destructive force. A massive collusion of water sources overwhelms: "Deep cries out to deep, the sounds of the opened sluices of heaven" so that "all Your breakers and Your billows have swept over me" (v. 8).

אוֹמְרָה לְאֵל סַלְעִי, לָמָה שְׁכַחְתָּנִי, ,
לָמָּה־קֹדֵר אֵלֵךְ בְּלַחַץ אוֹיֵב.
בְּרֶצַח בְּעַצְמוֹתַי חֵרְפוּנִי צוֹרְרָי, יא
בְּאָמְרָם אֵלַי כָּל־הַיּוֹם אַיֵּה אֱלֹהֶיךָ.
מַה־תִּשְׁתּוֹחֲחִי נַפְשִׁי, וּמַה־תֶּהֱמִי עָלָי; יב
הוֹחִילִי לֵאלֹהִים,
כִּי עוֹד־אוֹדֶנּוּ יְשׁוּעֹת פָּנַי וֵאלֹהָי.

I vividly recall my sense of helplessness as I received wave after wave of frightening information about my beloved's condition. The torrents of horrible news engulfed us. I remained helpless in the onslaught, feeling fragile, frightened, and abandoned, just like the psalmist.

In such distress, I could readily join our psalmist: "I say to the Almighty, my Rock, 'Why have you forsaken me? Why must I walk in dark gloom, oppressed by enemies?' Crushing my bones, my adversaries revile me, taunting me all day with, 'Where is your God?'" (vv. 10-11). During my period of tremendous loss, these lines expressed my inner voice with frightening precision.

Then, inevitably, I would be confronted by the last

10.   I say to the Almighty, my Rock:
              'Why have You forgotten me?
              'Why must I walk in dark gloom,
                oppressed by enemies?'

11. Crushing my bones
          my adversaries revile me,
          taunting me all day with,
             'Where is your God?'

12. Why so downcast, my soul?
          Why disquieted within me?
          Have hope in God!
             I will yet praise Him,
                my ever-present Help,
                my God.

verse of the psalm. Brief, almost terse, the solid faith reemerges: "Have hope in God; I will yet praise Him, my ever-present Help, my God" (v. 12).

What an unanticipated finale! How was the psalmist able to shift from a doubting "Where is your God?" to this declaration of faith in "my ever-present Help, my God"? What an incredible resolution!

This psalm may hint at the only possible response we can make to overwhelming pain and loss. The psalmist asks himself, "Why so downcast, my soul? Why disquieted within me?" His answer is instructive. Having poured his heart out, he does not deny the reality of his pain nor does he present simple pieties to explain God's design. Instead, in the face of adversity, he presents a human *response* rather than an *answer*.

The psalmist uses two words in the text that connect the faith of his past with hope for his future. In his concluding declaration of faith he says, *ki od*—"yet." This terminology suggests that, in the indefinite future, the exile will end. Although the current reality seems to preclude all reasonable hope, he reminds himself that there might yet be other options: "I will yet praise Him."

The glimmer of a more reassuring future is possible because of the power of memory of a joyous past. The word "praise" appears in this last verse—"I will yet praise Him"—and also appeared earlier in verse 5, where the author enjoyed his memory of celebrations in "the House of God with joyous shouts of praise." In the beginning of the psalm this word functioned as a reminder of the author's earlier relationship with God, one that he wishes to recall despite his exiled condition. By repeating that image at the end of the psalm, the author conjures up this earlier relationship and realizes that he may yet have these feelings in the future.

We may be so overwhelmed by a current reality that we seem to lack the strength to go on living. It is precisely at such times that our memory of past moments of connectedness, love, caring, closeness, and exultation must be invoked, not denied. In the face of overwhelming loss and fear for our future, we must call on those images from our past that give us moorings to face the future. By invoking the memory of past moments of divine praise, we may "yet" fulfill our thirst.

MY STRENGTH, MY HAVEN, MY FAITHFUL ONE

Introduction to Psalm 59

Rabbi Sheila Peltz Weinberg

THIS VERY PERSONAL PSALM CONTAINS THE CRIES OF SOMEONE searching for help in the face of life-threatening danger, beginning with a plea in despair and ending with a song of praise and thanksgiving. It moves from terror to serenity in a three-fold structure telescoped into a mere 18 lines.

The first verse sets the stage. David is fleeing Saul's wrath, running for his life. David is every person facing a relentless enemy, fighting for time, overwhelmed and over-powered by the superior force of the pursuer, be it illness, pain, weakness, isolation, or depression.

In verses 2-6, David, the poet, articulates several crucial thoughts. The very capacity to name what is happening, to call out for help, is an essential part of the transformation that occurs. The first call is shrill: "Save me! Save me! Rescue me! Help me!" Then the plight is described: "I am up against an enemy that is strong, evil, and capricious. I am truly innocent. God knows the truth that I am not the cause of my suffering. I will not add self-accusation and blame on top of my pain."

א לַמְנַצֵּחַ אַל־תַּשְׁחֵת, לְדָוִד מִכְתָּם;

בִּשְׁלֹחַ שָׁאוּל, וַיִּשְׁמְרוּ אֶת־הַבַּיִת לַהֲמִיתוֹ.

ב הַצִּילֵנִי מֵאֹיְבַי, אֱלֹהָי; מִמִּתְקוֹמְמַי תְּשַׂגְּבֵנִי.

ג הַצִּילֵנִי מִפֹּעֲלֵי אָוֶן וּמֵאַנְשֵׁי דָמִים הוֹשִׁיעֵנִי.

ד כִּי הִנֵּה אָרְבוּ לְנַפְשִׁי, יָגוּרוּ עָלַי עַזִּים;

לֹא־פִשְׁעִי וְלֹא־חַטָּאתִי, יהוה.

ה בְּלִי־עָוֹן יְרֻצוּן וְיִכּוֹנָנוּ, עוּרָה לִקְרָאתִי וּרְאֵה.

ו וְאַתָּה יהוה אֱלֹהִים צְבָאוֹת אֱלֹהֵי יִשְׂרָאֵל,

הָקִיצָה לִפְקֹד כָּל־הַגּוֹיִם,

אַל תָּחֹן כָּל־בֹּגְדֵי אָוֶן סֶלָה.

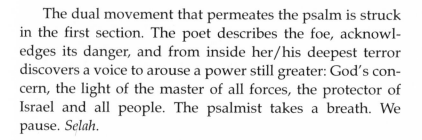

The dual movement that permeates the psalm is struck in the first section. The poet describes the foe, acknowledges its danger, and from inside her/his deepest terror discovers a voice to arouse a power still greater: God's concern, the light of the master of all forces, the protector of Israel and all people. The psalmist takes a breath. We pause. *Selah*.

PSALM 59

1. *To the Chief Musician, a precious song of David:*
   'Destroy not!'
   Composed when Saul sent messengers to surround
   David's house and kill him.
2. Rescue me from enemies, my God;
   from those who rise up against me—strengthen me!
3. Rescue me from those who act treacherously;
   from bloodthirsty people—save me!
4. For they lie in ambush for my soul,
   brazen ones gather against me;
   yet I have not transgressed,
   nor sinned against them, Adonai!
5. With no wrongdoing on my part,
   they run and prepare themselves—
   Awake, come towards me and see!
6. You, Adonai, God of Hosts,
   God of Israel,
   Rise up,
   Hold all peoples accountable;
   Show no favor to sinful traitors, *Selah.*

In the second section, verses 7-14, similar themes are struck. The nature of the enemy is described in more vivid terms, as growling, roving dogs. They stalk us in the evening, in the shadows of darkness, destroying our rest. Relentless in their hunger to consume us.

The terror has not abated, but the psalmist is learning how to identify the sounds and sights of the threat. He/she

ז יְשׁוּבוּ לָעֶרֶב, יֶהֱמוּ כַכָּלֶב, וִיסוֹבְבוּ עִיר.

ח הִנֵּה יַבִּיעוּן בְּפִיהֶם, חֲרָבוֹת בְּשִׂפְתוֹתֵיהֶם,
כִּי־מִי שֹׁמֵעַ.

ט וְאַתָּה יהוה תִּשְׂחַק־לָמוֹ, תִּלְעַג לְכָל־גּוֹיִם.

י עֻזּוֹ, אֵלֶיךָ אֶשְׁמֹרָה, כִּי־אֱלֹהִים מִשְׂגַּבִּי.

יא אֱלֹהֵי חַסְדִּי יְקַדְּמֵנִי, אֱלֹהִים יַרְאֵנִי בְשֹׁרְרָי.

יב אַל־תַּהַרְגֵם פֶּן־יִשְׁכְּחוּ עַמִּי;
הֲנִיעֵמוֹ בְחֵילְךָ וְהוֹרִידֵמוֹ, מָגִנֵּנוּ אֲדֹנָי.

יג חַטַּאת־פִּימוֹ דְּבַר־שְׂפָתֵימוֹ;
וְיִלָּכְדוּ בִגְאוֹנָם, וּמֵאָלָה וּמִכַּחַשׁ יְסַפֵּרוּ.

יד כַּלֵּה בְחֵמָה, כַּלֵּה וְאֵינֵמוֹ;
וְיֵדְעוּ כִּי־אֱלֹהִים מֹשֵׁל בְּיַעֲקֹב,
לְאַפְסֵי הָאָרֶץ סֶלָה.

also recognizes that the powerful foe is vulnerable and can
be mocked. Simultaneously, the poet is emboldened in
her/his relation to God. As the enemy is named and
acknowledged, so is God, source of help, strength, and
support. Three words appear in the Hebrew. Each word
as it is pronounced allows the suffering person to leap
across a chasm of hopelessness. The words are names of an

7. They return toward evening, howling like dogs,
  going round about the city;
8.   Mouths barking,
    swords in their lips,
    'Who hears it? Who cares?' they say.
9. But You, Adonai, You laugh at them,
  You scorn the evil among the nations.
10.   My Strength—
    for Your Help I wait,
    for God is my Haven.
11. God, my *Hessed*/Faithful One,
  You will go before me;
  God will let me gaze upon watchful foes.
12. Do not kill them, lest my people forget;
  remove them from prosperity, with Your power,
    and bring them down,
      our Shield, my Master.
13. For the sin of their mouth is the word of their lips,
  their very pride will trap them,
    because of the curses and lies that they tell.
14. Consume them in wrath;
  Consume them that they exist no more:
    and then they will know
      that God rules in Jacob
        to the ends of the earth, *Selah*.

intimate reservoir of help, an answer to the cries at the height of panic. The words are personal—*ozi*, My Strength, *misgavi*, My Haven, and *hasdi*, My Faithful One. As we name the unseen hands that cradle us in our most bereft moments, we can allow ourselves to lay some of our heavy burden in those hands. The psalmist takes a breath. We pause. *Selah*.

יז וְיָשֻׁבוּ לָעֶרֶב, יֶהֱמוּ כַכָּלֶב, וִיסוֹבְבוּ עִיר.

יז הֵמָּה יְנִיעוּן לֶאֱכֹל, אִם־לֹא יִשְׂבְּעוּ וַיָּלִינוּ.

יז וַאֲנִי אָשִׁיר עֻזֶּךָ, וַאֲרַנֵּן לַבֹּקֶר חַסְדֶּךָ;
כִּי־הָיִיתָ מִשְׂגָּב לִי, וּמָנוֹס בְּיוֹם צַר־לִי.

יח עֻזִּי אֵלֶיךָ אֲזַמֵּרָה; כִּי־אֱלֹהִים מִשְׂגַּבִּי,
אֱלֹהֵי חַסְדִּי.

The third and final section of the psalm, verses 15-18, begins with a repeated description of the vicious and unrelenting enemies. We hear their threatening sounds and see the bloodthirsty look in their eyes. Yet we do not blink. The poet, the person in pain, can now be fully present. The enemy has not dissolved, but we have been filled with an experience of God's care for us.

15. The wicked may return toward evening,
        howling like dogs,
        going round about the city;
16. wandering about, searching for food,
        they do not sleep until they are satiated.
17. But as for me
        I will sing of Your strength
        I will sing out loud in the morning,
            rejoicing in Your *Hessed*/Lovingkindness;
                for You have been my Stronghold,
                    a Refuge for me on my day of trouble.
18. My Strength—
        to You I will sing praises,
            for God is my Tower of Strength,
            God of my *Hessed*/Lovingkindness.

Our prayers have been answered in that the reality of God's loving strength has become a haven for us. We have entered into a refuge of faith and confidence which miraculously fills us with song. The battering of the enemy has been transformed through the magic of words, mere words, words that pass the tongue with great effort and reverberate to the highest heights.

THE ECHO OF YOUR PROMISE

Based on Psalm 77

Rabbi Harold M. Schulweis

When I cry my voice trembles with fear
When I call out it cracks with anger.

How can I greet the dawn with song
when darkness eclipses the rising sun

To whom shall I turn
when the clouds of the present eclipse the rays of
      tomorrow

Turn me around to yesterday
that I may be consoled by its memories.

Were not the seas split asunder
did we not once walk together through the waters
      to the dry side

Did we not bless the
bread that came forth from the heavens

עז

א לַמְנַצֵּחַ עַל־יְדוּתוּן לְאָסָף מִזְמוֹר.

ב קוֹלִי אֶל־אֱלֹהִים וְאֶצְעָקָה;

קוֹלִי אֶל־אֱלֹהִים, וְהַאֲזִין אֵלָי.

ג בְּיוֹם צָרָתִי אֲדֹנָי דָּרָשְׁתִּי;

יָדִי לַיְלָה נִגְּרָה וְלֹא תָפוּג, מֵאֲנָה הִנָּחֵם נַפְשִׁי.

ד אֶזְכְּרָה אֱלֹהִים וְאֶהֱמָיָה,

אָשִׂיחָה וְתִתְעַטֵּף רוּחִי סֶלָה.

ה אָחַזְתָּ שְׁמֻרוֹת עֵינָי, נִפְעַמְתִּי וְלֹא אֲדַבֵּר.

ו חִשַּׁבְתִּי יָמִים מִקֶּדֶם, שְׁנוֹת עוֹלָמִים.

ז אֶזְכְּרָה נְגִינָתִי בַּלָּיְלָה;

עִם־לְבָבִי אָשִׂיחָה, וַיְחַפֵּשׂ רוּחִי.

ח הַלְעוֹלָמִים יִזְנַח l אֲדֹנָי, וְלֹא־יֹסִיף לִרְצוֹת עוֹד.

Did your voice not reach my ears
and direct my wanderings

The waters, the lightning, the thunder
remind me of yesterday's triumphs

Let the past offer proof of tomorrow
let it be my comforter and guarantor.

PSALM 77

1. *To the Chief Musician:*
   On the sufferings of evil decrees; A song of Asaph.
2. I lift my voice to God and cry out;
       I lift my voice to God
       and He turns His ears to hear.
3. On my day of suffering
       I seek out my Master;
       At night, my hand reaches out,
           without ceasing;
               My soul refuses to be comforted.
4. I remember God—and I moan;
       When I talk,
           my spirit faints, Selah.
5. You gripped the lids of my eyes;
       I throbbed in pain, and could not speak.
6. I recall former days—
       ancient years, time long past;
7.   I remember my song, well into the night;
       I delve into my heart,
       My spirit searches and seeks.
8.   Will my Master cast me off forever?
       Will He not show favor to me once again?

I have been here before
known the fright and found your companionship.

I enter the sanctuary again
to await the echo of your promise.

ט הֶאָפֵס לָנֶצַח חַסְדּוֹ, גָּמַר אֹמֶר לְדֹר וָדֹר.

י הֲשָׁכַח חַנּוֹת אֵל, אִם־קָפַץ בְּאַף רַחֲמָיו סֶלָה.

יא וָאֹמַר חַלּוֹתִי הִיא, שְׁנוֹת יְמִין עֶלְיוֹן.

יב אֶזְכּוֹר מַעַלְלֵי־יָהּ, כִּי־אֶזְכְּרָה מִקֶּדֶם פִּלְאֶךָ.

יג וְהָגִיתִי בְכָל־פָּעֳלֶךָ, וּבַעֲלִילוֹתֶיךָ אָשִׂיחָה.

יד אֱלֹהִים בַּקֹּדֶשׁ דַּרְכֶּךָ, מִי אֵל גָּדוֹל כֵּאלֹהִים.

טו אַתָּה הָאֵל עֹשֵׂה פֶלֶא, הוֹדַעְתָּ בָעַמִּים עֻזֶּךָ.

טז גָּאַלְתָּ בִּזְרוֹעַ עַמֶּךָ, בְּנֵי־יַעֲקֹב וְיוֹסֵף סֶלָה.

יז רָאוּךָ מַּיִם אֱלֹהִים, רָאוּךָ מַּיִם יָחִילוּ,
אַף יִרְגְּזוּ תְהֹמוֹת.

יח זֹרְמוּ מַיִם עָבוֹת, קוֹל נָתְנוּ שְׁחָקִים,
אַף־חֲצָצֶיךָ יִתְהַלָּכוּ.

יט קוֹל רַעַמְךָ בַּגַּלְגַּל, הֵאִירוּ בְרָקִים תֵּבֵל,
רָגְזָה וַתִּרְעַשׁ הָאָרֶץ.

כ בַּיָּם דַּרְכֶּךָ, וּשְׁבִילְךָ בְּמַיִם רַבִּים,
וְעִקְּבוֹתֶיךָ לֹא נֹדָעוּ.

כא נָחִיתָ כַצֹּאן עַמֶּךָ, בְּיַד־מֹשֶׁה וְאַהֲרֹן.

9.   Has His *Hessed*/Lovingkindness disappeared once
and for all?
     Has His word come to an end—
     for all generations?

10.   Has the Almighty forgotten how to be gracious?
     Has His anger shut out His mercy, *Selah*?

11. I said, 'It is to terrify me, to inspire me with fear,
     that the Right Hand of the Most High has
     shifted.'

12. I remember the deeds of God,
     I remember Your wonders from days long ago.

13.   I meditate on all Your work, Your actions,
     I speak of Your deeds.

14. God: Holiness is Your way—
     What power is as great as God?

15. You are the Almighty who does wonders,
     You have let all nations know of Your strength.

16. You redeemed Your people with an outstretched arm,
     the children of Jacob and Joseph, *Selah*.

17. The waters saw you, God,
     the waters saw you and were terrified;
     The depths trembled in turmoil!

18. The clouds poured out water,
     the skies emitted thunderclaps,
     Your hailstone arrows flew about!

19. The sound of Your thunder
     whirled out like a wheel,
     Bolts of lightning illumined the world,
     the earth trembled and quaked.

20. Your way was in the sea
     Your path was in the great waters
     Your footsteps were not visible.

21. You led Your people as a flock,
     by the hand of Moses and Aaron.

CRISIS AND CONFIDENCE

Introduction to Psalm 90

Rabbi Eugene B. Borowitz

OUR LIVES TEND TO SHIFT BETWEEN TWO MOODS. I DO NOT MEAN dramatic swings between great elation or deep dejection, but rather the simple shifts that are part of the quiet rhythm of the everyday. They raise us from the stability of routine to a warm feeling of confidence, or lower us into doubting that anything really matters or is worth our effort.

Our psalm speaks to me of this alternation of temper. We begin it confidently enough. After all, it is a psalm, part of our sacred literature, something Jews have recited for millennia and perhaps familiar from the early part of the Shabbat morning service. It announces itself—quite uniquely—as "A prayer of Moses, the man of God." If Moses could say this, then surely we will benefit from his words. And, like all good prayers, it reminds us "before Whom we stand," as the common synagogue ark wall motto has it. We turn to God, this time addressed as the Ever-was-and-Enduring-One who has been a lasting source of help to us (vv. 1-2). This description of God's deathlessness initially seems only a basic expression of trust, but it will soon return, with a rather ominous shift, exactly as a mood swing does, to us.

צ

א תְּפִלָּה לְמֹשֶׁה אִישׁ־הָאֱלֹהִים:

אֲדֹנָי, מָעוֹן אַתָּה הָיִיתָ לָּנוּ בְּדֹר וָדֹר.

ב בְּטֶרֶם הָרִים יֻלָּדוּ,

וַתְּחוֹלֵל אֶרֶץ וְתֵבֵל,

וּמֵעוֹלָם עַד־עוֹלָם אַתָּה אֵל.

ג תָּשֵׁב אֱנוֹשׁ עַד דַּכָּא, וַתֹּאמֶר: שׁוּבוּ בְנֵי־אָדָם.

ד כִּי אֶלֶף שָׁנִים בְּעֵינֶיךָ כְּיוֹם אֶתְמוֹל כִּי יַעֲבֹר,

וְאַשְׁמוּרָה בַלָּיְלָה.

ה זְרַמְתָּם, שֵׁנָה יִהְיוּ, בַּבֹּקֶר כֶּחָצִיר יַחֲלֹף.

For beginning in verse 3 a more troubling tone appears. God wants us to stop taking ourselves and our accomplishments so seriously. Looking back now on the accomplishments we worked so hard for over the years, what happened to them? What were they really worth? Can we even remember all the things that we were once so intense about—or took such care to evade? And if we still esteem them, what really do they amount to in God's "eyes" for whom "a thousand years...are like yesterday...like a watch in the night," "a flood," "a sleep," or the overnight grass (vv. 4-6)? Useless, all useless; empty, all empty. A sigh rises from the soul.

PSALM 90

1. A prayer of Moses, a man of God:
   Adonai, You have been a refuge for us
   in every generation.
2. Before the mountains were born,
   before You brought forth the earth and the
                          inhabited world,
   from world to world—
   You are the Almighty.
3. You bring people down
   from arrogance to contrition;
   You say,
   'Return to Me, children of Adam and Eve!'
4. For a thousand years are in Your eyes
   like yesterday, which has just passed,
   like a watch in the night.
5. The stream of human life is like a dream;
   In the morning, it is as grass, sprouting fresh;

   The mood intensifies, moving on now to what we see as the cause of our dis-ease: God's anger, fiercely executing God's justice (vv. 7-9). For we cannot stand before God claiming to be wholly righteous and thus worthy of God's good gifts: Life, health, and all that properly goes with them. In simple truth, we haven't done all God wanted us to do—and though we can't think of anything so terrible that we did, we are reminded that God knows even our "hidden misdeeds" (v. 8). So, in a bitter charge, the psalm says all our life, brief as it is, has been permeated by God's wrath. Surely there are people whose lives have been an unending succession of tragedies.

בַּבֹּקֶר יָצִיץ וְחָלָף, לָעֶרֶב יְמוֹלֵל וְיָבֵשׁ. ו

כִּי־כָלִינוּ בְאַפֶּךָ, וּבַחֲמָתְךָ נִבְהָלְנוּ. ז

שַׁתָּ עֲוֹנֹתֵינוּ לְנֶגְדֶּךָ, עֲלֻמֵנוּ לִמְאוֹר פָּנֶיךָ. ח

כִּי כָל־יָמֵינוּ פָּנוּ בְעֶבְרָתֶךָ, כִּלִּינוּ שָׁנֵינוּ כְמוֹ־הֶגֶה. ט

יְמֵי־שְׁנוֹתֵינוּ בָהֶם שִׁבְעִים שָׁנָה, י

וְאִם בִּגְבוּרֹת שְׁמוֹנִים שָׁנָה,

וְרָהְבָּם עָמָל וָאָוֶן, כִּי־גָז חִישׁ וַנָּעֻפָה.

מִי־יוֹדֵעַ עֹז אַפֶּךָ, וּכְיִרְאָתְךָ עֶבְרָתֶךָ. יא

לִמְנוֹת יָמֵינוּ כֵּן הוֹדַע, וְנָבִא לְבַב חָכְמָה. יב

Despair threatens to overwhelm us—but even as we feel that, another thought arises in us: This is a prayer of Moses. "The man of God" may fearlessly acknowledge the aching sense of human transitoriness, but he does not lose hope. And, so we trust, neither will we, praying a "Prayer of Moses."

A subtle hint of confidence now asserts itself, that the human lifespan is seventy years, occasionally eighty—no small matter when the average child born in biblical times was lucky to make it to thirty-five (v. 10). The numbers are comforting and remind us of what often happens. But the numbers will not magically banish all our momentary

6. In the morning, it blossoms and flourishes;
    but by evening, it is cut down and shrivels.
7. So are we consumed by Your anger;
    we are terrified by Your rage.
8. You have placed our sins before You;
    Our hidden misdeeds
        are exposed by the light of Your countenance.
9. All our days vanish
        in the glare of Your wrath;
    We have used up our years,
        which pass like a word unspoken.
10. The days of our years may total seventy;
        if we are exceptionally strong, perhaps eighty;
        but all their pride and glory is toil and
            falsehood,
        and, severed quickly, we fly away.
11. Who can know the force of Your fury?
        Your rage is as awful as our fear!
12. To count every day—teach us,
        so we will acquire a heart of wisdom.

feelings of loss and deprivation. There is too much about their caustic realism that is true. Life can easily grind us down and before we know what has happened it has flown away. When this distemper seizes us, we see God as very fierce and unrelenting indeed (vv. 10-11).

Is it too modern to say that all this harshness ascribed to God may, underneath, say more about us than God? We are angry, mad that another trouble has come upon us. But now the several references to our sins are highly suggestive. Perhaps we are particularly sensitive because we fear that our inattention or misdeeds may make us partly (largely?) responsible for putting us in harm's way.

יג שׁוּבָה יהוה עַד־מָתָי, וְהִנָּחֵם עַל־עֲבָדֶיךָ.

יד שַׂבְּעֵנוּ בַבֹּקֶר חַסְדֶּךָ, וּנְרַנְּנָה וְנִשְׂמְחָה בְּכָל־יָמֵינוּ.

טו שַׂמְּחֵנוּ כִּימוֹת עִנִּיתָנוּ, שְׁנוֹת רָאִינוּ רָעָה.

טז יֵרָאֶה אֶל־עֲבָדֶיךָ פָעֳלֶךָ, וַהֲדָרְךָ עַל־בְּנֵיהֶם.

יז וִיהִי נֹעַם אֲדֹנָי אֱלֹהֵינוּ עָלֵינוּ,
וּמַעֲשֵׂה יָדֵינוּ כּוֹנְנָה עָלֵינוּ,
וּמַעֲשֵׂה יָדֵינוּ כּוֹנְנֵהוּ.

Acknowledging these very deep, disturbing feelings—
which confess our possible complicity in what has happened—doesn't turn life into a yellow-brick road to dance
down. But it helps us distinguish our passions from our
sober sense of God's nature. In any case, this emotional dis-
charge has had one effect, for the poem's tone now
changes. To begin with, we admit that maybe we might
learn something from all of this. As we say, "If I ever get
over this, I'll be a different person" (v. 12). Then, too, we
find ourselves hopeful enough to ask God quickly to turn
our tears to joy and keep us untroubled in the future (v. 14)
or at least to compensate us for all our suffering (v. 15).

13. Return, Adonai—how long?
> Take pity, have compassion on Your servants.
14. Satisfy us in the morning
> with Your *Hessed*/Lovingkindness,
> and we will sing and rejoice all our days!
15. Give us joy
> that will challenge the days of our affliction,
>> the years we have seen evil.
16. Let Your work be revealed to Your servants,
> let Your splendor be on their children.
17. May the pleasantness of my Master, our God, rest
> upon us,
> and may the work of our hands be established;
> Establish the work of our hands!

More, we'd like all that love and kindness we have known from God to be manifest, not just to us but to our children as well (v. 16). And, since we must not forget how ephemeral we really are, we ask God to invest our striving with some of God's own enduring power. Yes, all things considered, we are again quietly confident about life and its promise—as long as we have God's help. Once more we say, "God, establish the word of our hands" (v. 17).

Will our prayer be answered? That is for God to determine. But in one sense, it already has been, for we end this prayer different from when we started it.

BREAKING THE SPIRITUAL GRIDLOCK

An Introduction to Psalm 105

Rabbi Maurice Lamm

IF WE ARE GOING TO HEAL FROM ILLNESS WE NEED TO BREAK TWO kinds of spiritual gridlock. One paralyzes us so that we become passive and resigned; the other steals the very song from our throats, leaving us with only a groan. The spirit evaporates from our souls and we become submissive and flat. Psalm 105 teaches two positive ways to heal, and healing is the essence of health.

First, when illness de-activates us, we follow a prepared script and act like victims—we become couch potatoes, helplessly watching ourselves get weaker. We are fed and injected and analyzed and tested and predicted and watched over and prayed for and spoken of behind our backs. It is a gridlock that paralyzes us and makes us feel worse. Psalm 105 tells us: "Don't act like a victim."

Notice how the psalmist erupts and fires off ten staccato charges in five sentences—give thanks; call Him, make known His works; sing to him; praise Him; speak of Him; glory in Him; search for His presence; seek Him; remember Him! To heal, to become whole, we must respond even ten

א הוֹדוּ לַיהוה קִרְאוּ בִשְׁמוֹ,
הוֹדִיעוּ בָעַמִּים עֲלִילוֹתָיו.

ב שִׁירוּ־לוֹ זַמְּרוּ־לוֹ, שִׂיחוּ בְּכָל־נִפְלְאוֹתָיו.

ג הִתְהַלְלוּ בְּשֵׁם קָדְשׁוֹ, יִשְׂמַח לֵב מְבַקְשֵׁי יהוה.

ד דִּרְשׁוּ יהוה וְעֻזּוֹ, בַּקְּשׁוּ פָנָיו תָּמִיד.

ה זִכְרוּ נִפְלְאוֹתָיו אֲשֶׁר־עָשָׂה, מֹפְתָיו וּמִשְׁפְּטֵי־פִיו.

ו זֶרַע אַבְרָהָם עַבְדּוֹ, בְּנֵי יַעֲקֹב בְּחִירָיו.

ז הוּא יהוה אֱלֹהֵינוּ, בְּכָל־הָאָרֶץ מִשְׁפָּטָיו.

ח זָכַר לְעוֹלָם בְּרִיתוֹ, דָּבָר צִוָּה לְאֶלֶף דּוֹר.

---

times; energize our minds; and not allow ourselves to sink into victimhood.

Pain focuses our mind marvelously, a thinker once said. It will require heroism to take our mind off our condition, to take control of our souls, to be courageous, to feel empowered again. You may say: "I can't think of anything else." Perhaps you can't, but try it. I urge you to keep your mind active on other subjects. Your brain does have a mind of its own—but you can control it. Times like these call for combat, not resignation.

PSALM 105

1. Give thanks to Adonai, call upon His name;
   Let all nations know about His deeds!
2. Sing to Him, compose songs, play instruments for
   Him;
   Tell all about His wondrous acts!
3. Take pride in His Holy Name;
   The heart of those who seek Him rejoices!
4. Search for Adonai and for His might,
   Seek His presence always!
5. Remember the wonders He has performed,
   His miracles, and the laws from His mouth.
6. Seed of Abraham His servant,
   Children of Jacob, His chosen:
7. He is Adonai, our God;
   The whole earth is governed by His laws.
8. He remembered His eternal covenant,
   the word which He commanded to a thousand
   generations.

Now break the second gridlock. In the ten charges of the psalmist, one appears not to fit—"Sing to Him!" What's the value of a song? In our sophistication, we think of singing as an art form; but the Torah teaches that to sing is a blessing. In terms of the spirit, singing is on a higher level than speaking—it is why the Levites sang in the Temple. The word *shir*, meaning song, also derives from *shur*, meaning insight. When we sing we raise our souls to God, and we gain insight into Him. Through song we address God.

And through song we learn to better endure our

אֲשֶׁר כָּרַת אֶת־אַבְרָהָם, וּשְׁבוּעָתוֹ לְיִשְׂחָק. ט

וַיַּעֲמִידֶהָ לְיַעֲקֹב לְחֹק, לְיִשְׂרָאֵל בְּרִית עוֹלָם. י

לֵאמֹר לְךָ אֶתֵּן אֶת־אֶרֶץ־כְּנָעַן, חֶבֶל נַחֲלַתְכֶם. יא

בִּהְיוֹתָם מְתֵי מִסְפָּר, כִּמְעַט וְגָרִים בָּהּ. יב

וַיִּתְהַלְכוּ מִגּוֹי אֶל־גּוֹי, מִמַּמְלָכָה אֶל־עַם אַחֵר. יג

לֹא־הִנִּיחַ אָדָם לְעָשְׁקָם, וַיּוֹכַח עֲלֵיהֶם מְלָכִים. יד

אַל־תִּגְּעוּ בִמְשִׁיחָי, וְלִנְבִיאַי אַל־תָּרֵעוּ. טו

וַיִּקְרָא רָעָב עַל־הָאָרֶץ, כָּל־מַטֵּה־לֶחֶם שָׁבָר. טז

שָׁלַח לִפְנֵיהֶם אִישׁ, לְעֶבֶד נִמְכַּר יוֹסֵף. יז

עִנּוּ בַכֶּבֶל רַגְלוֹ, בַּרְזֶל בָּאָה נַפְשׁוֹ. יח

---

hardships. When life is not a song, sing! When King David
was ill, he sang; when Cervantes, the great writer, was ill,
he said: "He who sings frightens away his ills." Ask yourself: Why do people always smile when they sing? Singing
is an antidote to panic. The Hasidim taught us that. It light-
ens the burden, lessens the fear, steadies the nerves.
Singing gives voice to our deepest feelings; it enables us to
express ourselves even if we are the only ones who hear it.
And we will have made ourselves heard. Singing lifts the
heart.

9. The covenant which He made with Abraham,
        His oath to Isaac—
10. He established it as a statute for Jacob,
        for Israel—an everlasting covenant.
11. Saying,
        "To you I will give the land of Canaan,
            the portion of your inheritance."
12. When they were only few in number,
        and had scarcely dwelled in the land;
13. when they wandered from nation to nation,
        from one kingdom to another people—
14. He permitted no one to oppress them;
        He admonished kings on their behalf:
15.   "Do not touch My anointed ones,
            and to My prophets do no harm."
16. He called a famine in the land,
        their staff of life, their bread, He broke off.
17. Before them He sent a man—
        Joseph, sold as a slave.
18. They weighed his legs down in fetters,
        an iron chain on his soul.

Even if all we do is chant "Oy Vay," over and over, to a tune we improvise—*Shiru lo*, "Sing to Him." Even a melancholy song somehow takes us out of ourselves and gives expression to our inner being. Sometimes I break out in a *niggun*—a melody that uses sounds shaped only by my emotions. It articulates a groan that forces its way out of my interior; sometimes, it expresses an indescribable joy inside me that's in search of an audience.

Sometimes we sing a familiar *niggun* with friends with whom we sway in oneness. It crystallizes our common

יט עַד־עֵת בֹּא־דְבָרוֹ, אִמְרַת יהוה צְרָפָתְהוּ.

כ שָׁלַח מֶלֶךְ וַיַּתִּירֵהוּ, מֹשֵׁל עַמִּים וַיְפַתְּחֵהוּ.

כא שָׂמוֹ אָדוֹן לְבֵיתוֹ, וּמֹשֵׁל בְּכָל־קִנְיָנוֹ.

כב לֶאְסֹר שָׂרָיו בְּנַפְשׁוֹ, וּזְקֵנָיו יְחַכֵּם.

כג וַיָּבֹא יִשְׂרָאֵל מִצְרָיִם, וְיַעֲקֹב גָּר בְּאֶרֶץ־חָם.

כד וַיֶּפֶר אֶת־עַמּוֹ מְאֹד, וַיַּעֲצִמֵהוּ מִצָּרָיו.

כה הָפַךְ לִבָּם לִשְׂנֹא עַמּוֹ, לְהִתְנַכֵּל בַּעֲבָדָיו.

כו שָׁלַח מֹשֶׁה עַבְדּוֹ, אַהֲרֹן אֲשֶׁר בָּחַר־בּוֹ.

כז שָׂמוּ־בָם דִּבְרֵי אֹתוֹתָיו, וּמֹפְתִים בְּאֶרֶץ חָם.

כח שָׁלַח חֹשֶׁךְ וַיַּחְשִׁךְ, וְלֹא מָרוּ אֶת דְּבָרוֹ.

despair, and the sadness gets dissipated in fellowship. It harmonizes our own souls with the souls of those who empathize with us. The harmony, in magical ways, transfers the energy of the group to us fragile individuals as we lift up our voices and keep time together.

Sing what you like; help others by offering to sing with them. Especially effective may be a mother's *niggun*, one that she sang for us at bedtime or when we were sick. We can sing from religious songs; old nursery rhymes; oldies but goodies; college songs—if they make us smile or help

19. Until His word came to pass,
     the word of Adonai purified him.
20. The king sent messengers and released him,
     the ruler of many peoples set him free.
21. He appointed him master over his house,
     ruler over all his possessions,
22.   binding his ministers to his soul,
        making his elders wise.
23. Israel then came down to Egypt,
     Jacob sojourned in the land of Ham.
24. God made His people extremely fruitful,
     He made them stronger than their adversaries,
25.   whose hearts He turned to hate His people,
        to conspire against His servants.
26. He sent Moses, His servant,
     and Aaron, whom He had chosen.
27. They performed among them
     words of His signs,
        wonders in the land of Ham.
28. He sent darkness—and it was dark;
     they did not rebel against His word.

---

us to express our anxiety. If you feel the onset of despair, sing out your despair in a *niggun*.

To groan when we are ill is common; to sing is courageous. Think actively, sing passionately. It will break the most common gridlocks of illness, and let our souls soar to new heights.

כט הָפַךְ אֶת־מֵימֵיהֶם לְדָם, וַיָּמֶת אֶת־דְּגָתָם.

ל שָׁרַץ אַרְצָם צְפַרְדְּעִים, בְּחַדְרֵי מַלְכֵיהֶם.

לא אָמַר וַיָּבֹא עָרֹב, כִּנִּים בְּכָל־גְּבוּלָם.

לב נָתַן גִּשְׁמֵיהֶם בָּרָד, אֵשׁ לֶהָבוֹת בְּאַרְצָם.

לג וַיַּךְ גַּפְנָם וּתְאֵנָתָם, וַיְשַׁבֵּר עֵץ גְּבוּלָם.

לד אָמַר וַיָּבֹא אַרְבֶּה, וְיֶלֶק וְאֵין מִסְפָּר.

לה וַיֹּאכַל כָּל־עֵשֶׂב בְּאַרְצָם, וַיֹּאכַל פְּרִי אַדְמָתָם.

לו וַיַּךְ כָּל־בְּכוֹר בְּאַרְצָם, רֵאשִׁית לְכָל־אוֹנָם.

לז וַיּוֹצִיאֵם בְּכֶסֶף וְזָהָב, וְאֵין בִּשְׁבָטָיו כּוֹשֵׁל.

לח שָׂמַח מִצְרַיִם בְּצֵאתָם, כִּי־נָפַל פַּחְדָּם עֲלֵיהֶם.

לט פָּרַשׂ עָנָן לְמָסָךְ, וְאֵשׁ לְהָאִיר לָיְלָה.

מ שָׁאַל וַיָּבֵא שְׂלָו, וְלֶחֶם שָׁמַיִם יַשְׂבִּיעֵם.

מא פָּתַח צוּר וַיָּזוּבוּ מָיִם, הָלְכוּ בַּצִּיּוֹת נָהָר.

מב כִּי־זָכַר אֶת דְּבַר קָדְשׁוֹ, אֶת־אַבְרָהָם עַבְדּוֹ.

מג וַיּוֹצִא עַמּוֹ בְשָׂשׂוֹן, בְּרִנָּה אֶת־בְּחִירָיו.

מד וַיִּתֵּן לָהֶם אַרְצוֹת גּוֹיִם, וַעֲמַל לְאֻמִּים יִירָשׁוּ.

מה בַּעֲבוּר יִשְׁמְרוּ חֻקָּיו, וְתוֹרֹתָיו יִנְצֹרוּ, הַלְלוּיָהּ.

29. He turned their waters into blood,
      causing their fish to die.
30. Their land swarmed with frogs,
      reaching the very chambers of the kings.
31. He spoke, and wild beasts came,
      lice throughout their borders.
32. He turned their rains into hail,
      flaming fire in their land.
33.   The hail struck their vines and fig trees,
      shattered the trees within their borders.
34. God spoke and locusts came,
      beetles beyond number.
35.   They ate every herb in their land,
      they devoured the fruit of their soil.
36. He struck all the firstborn in their land,
      the prime of their strength.
37. He brought them out, carrying silver and gold,
      and none among His tribes stumbled.
38. Egypt rejoiced when they departed,
      for their terror had fallen upon them.
39. He spread out a cloud as a sheltering cover,
      a fire to illumine the night.
40. Israel asked and He provided quail,
      He satisfied them with bread from Heaven.
41. He broke open a rock and waters gushed out,
      rushing through dry places like a river.
42. For He remembered His holy word, His promise
      to Abraham, His servant.
43. He brought out His people with gladness,
      His chosen ones with joyful singing.
44. He gave them the lands of nations,
      they inherited that which nations acquire by
            labor.
45. So that they might keep His statutes,
      and treasure His teachings,
            Halleluyah!

I MUST KEEP SINGING

Introduction to Psalm 137

Rabbi Amy Eilberg

"By the rivers of Babylon,
there we sat and we wept
as we remembered Zion."

SOMETIMES THERE IS NOTHING TO DO BUT WEEP. MY BODY ISN'T working. I can't even find my spirit. I feel so foggy, so burdened, so scared, in so much pain; I feel as if I'm in exile. I can't find my way back home. Where is home, anyway, right now? I allow myself to lie down and cry.

I had always read Psalm 137 only in historical terms, the homesick lament of the Jews in exile in Babylon, weeping for Jerusalem, their home. But to read the psalm through Rabbi Nachman's eyes is to imagine the lament as my own, as a cry of despair and longing in my own times of pain and lostness and confusion, when I am disoriented, forcibly removed from the normal, comfortable times and places of my life. Rabbi Nachman invites us to read the psalm as our own cry, our own prayer, inviting us to move, as the psalm does, from despair to joy and power.

א עַל־נַהֲרוֹת בָּבֶל, שָׁם יָשַׁבְנוּ גַּם־בָּכִינוּ,
בְּזָכְרֵנוּ אֶת־צִיּוֹן.

ב עַל־עֲרָבִים בְּתוֹכָהּ, תָּלִינוּ כִּנֹּרוֹתֵינוּ.

ג כִּי שָׁם שְׁאֵלוּנוּ שׁוֹבֵינוּ דִּבְרֵי־שִׁיר וְתוֹלָלֵינוּ שִׂמְחָה,
שִׁירוּ לָנוּ מִשִּׁיר צִיּוֹן.

ד אֵיךְ נָשִׁיר אֶת־שִׁיר־יְהוָה, עַל אַדְמַת נֵכָר.

ה אִם־אֶשְׁכָּחֵךְ יְרוּשָׁלָם, תִּשְׁכַּח יְמִינִי.

ו תִּדְבַּק לְשׁוֹנִי לְחִכִּי, אִם־לֹא אֶזְכְּרֵכִי,
אִם־לֹא אַעֲלֶה אֶת־יְרוּשָׁלַם עַל רֹאשׁ שִׂמְחָתִי.

DESPAIR: VERSES 1-4

I am in exile. Nothing is normal, nothing is familiar, nothing is as it should be. I remember better times, when life was easier, when I thought I knew just where I was going, when the future seemed wide open before me. Now, my body's not working, and so everything is changed. I don't know this territory, don't know what to do or where to go. Sometimes I just want to get out of here. I twist and turn and struggle, trying to find my way out of the confusion, out of the darkness. How can I even use the things that once brought me comfort? I can't even remember them. Sometimes I can't even let in the people who used to bring

Psalm 137

1. By the rivers of Babylon,
   there we sat and we wept
   as we remembered Zion.
2. Upon the willows on its banks
   we hung up our harps.
3. For there our captors demanded of us
   words of song;
   Our tormentors asked of us (with) joy:
   'Sing to us from the songs of Zion!'
4. But how shall we sing the song of Adonai
   on alien soil?
5. If I ever forget you, Jerusalem,
   may my right hand forget its cunning!
6. May my tongue cleave to the roof of my mouth,
   if I remember you not;
   if I do not set Jerusalem
   above my highest joy!

me joy. How can I possibly sing my old songs? How do I go on? I just allow myself to cry.

Joy: Verses 5-6

Then, suddenly, something shifts. I see a ray of light. I notice what is working. For a moment, I am so glad to be here. I can sing after all. I can sing songs of gratitude, even now. Just for a moment, I notice what is working in my body, in my life. I am breathing, I am here. The sun is still shining. I still have things to do. I am still me. I am alive.

I must keep singing this song of peace, even if I can only do it a moment a day. I must keep singing, or I will

זְכֹר יְהוָה לִבְנֵי אֱדוֹם אֵת יוֹם יְרוּשָׁלָםִ; הָאֹמְרִים עָרוּ עָרוּ, עַד הַיְסוֹד בָּהּ.

בַּת בָּבֶל הַשְּׁדוּדָה, אַשְׁרֵי שֶׁיְשַׁלֶּם־לָךְ אֶת־גְּמוּלֵךְ שֶׁגָּמַלְתְּ לָנוּ.

אַשְׁרֵי שֶׁיֹּאחֵז וְנִפֵּץ אֶת־עֹלָלַיִךְ אֶל־הַסָּלַע.

lose everything. I won't let my hands stop reaching out. I won't let my words stop expressing who I am. I will use my hands, to act as I still can. I will use my tongue, to say what I still need to say. I will not be defeated by despair. Even if just for moments at a time, I will keep singing the song of life.

POWER: VERSES 7-9

For a moment, I feel strong. I am fighting a powerful enemy that threatens my body and spirit. But I know that I am not alone. O God, I dare to believe that You stand with

7. Remind the sons of Edom, Adonai, about the
                    day of Jerusalem—
         Remind those who said,
              'Raze it, raze it to its very foundation!'
8. Daughter of Babylon,
         it is you who are the annihilated one;
              Happy is the one who will repay you
                   for all that you have done to us!
9. Happy is the one who will grab *your* little
                    ones,
         dashing them against the rock!

me in this trial. I believe You want me to win—whatever that may mean, that You want for me to bring all my strength to living with this. Promise me that You will bless me in the midst of this, that You will guide me to the treasure that may be hidden for me within this struggle.

O God, rage with me against this enemy. Be with me in my anger. Remember that I am Your child. Help me as I fight to live as fully as I can through this. Be my support, my courage, my strength. Hold me when I fall, love me when I doubt, cheer me on when I have moments of triumph. Dear God, with You on my side, I can go on.

PRAISE, JOY, BREATH

Introduction to Psalm 150

Rabbi Nancy Flam

PRAISE

How can one praise God in the midst of serious illness?
Praise God for one's situation not being worse? What if it is
nearly as bad as one can imagine? Praise God for the memory of health? What if one was born with a congenital dis-
ease? Praise God for the depth of experience and insight
which can come through suffering? Who wouldn't trade a
little insight for a modicum of relief?

The psalm says, "Praise God for God's mighty deeds;
praise God according to God's abundant greatness." What
are these mighty deeds, this abundant greatness? The
poem is vague; I do not know the author's intention. But I
do know that what one considers God's "greatness" will
depend upon one's understanding of God's nature and
ways.

The mighty deeds might refer to God's intervening in
history: Performing miracles such as splitting the Red Sea.
Personally, I cannot conceive of God this way: A power
who willfully changes the laws of nature to help a particular

קנ

א הַלְלוּיָהּ, הַלְלוּ־אֵל בְּקָדְשׁוֹ,
הַלְלוּהוּ בִּרְקִיעַ עֻזּוֹ.
ב הַלְלוּהוּ בִגְבוּרֹתָיו, הַלְלוּהוּ כְּרֹב גֻּדְלוֹ.
ג הַלְלוּהוּ בְּתֵקַע שׁוֹפָר, הַלְלוּהוּ בְּנֵבֶל וְכִנּוֹר.
ד הַלְלוּהוּ בְתֹף וּמָחוֹל, הַלְלוּהוּ בְּמִנִּים וְעֻגָב.
ה הַלְלוּהוּ בְצִלְצְלֵי־שָׁמַע,
הַלְלוּהוּ בְּצִלְצְלֵי תְרוּעָה.
ו כֹּל הַנְּשָׁמָה תְּהַלֵּל יָהּ, הַלְלוּיָהּ.

people. But I do affirm and praise God as the One who makes miracles everyday, according to the laws of the physical universe and the human spirit: The awesome power we sense as we witness fall turn to winter, and winter to spring; the One we feel when we experience true love and compassion; who has willed the natural cycle of growth and decay; in whose presence we find company in prayer.

Such greatness pertains whether I am ill or well. Praise of God is not about me or my condition; it is about the reality of God.

Psalm 150

1. *Halleluyah*/Praise God!
     Praise God in His Sanctuary;
     Praise Him
          in the vast expanse of Heaven!
2. Praise Him for mighty deeds;
     Praise Him
          according to His abundant greatness!
3. Praise Him
     with the blowing of the *shofar*;
          Praise Him
               with the lyre and the harp!
4. Praise Him
     with drum and dance;
          Praise Him
               with string instruments and flute!
5. Praise Him
     with resounding cymbals!
          Praise Him
               with clanging cymbals!
6. Let every breath of life praise God,
     Halleluyah/Praise God!

Joy

It may require a psycho-spiritual tour de force to praise
God with joy and gladness in the midst of illness, but Rabbi
Nachman challenges us to do so. Psalm 150 is nothing
short of ecstatic, a glorious symphony which rises to a daz-
zling crescendo: Shofar blasts, harp and lyre, timbrel,
dance, lute and pipe, cymbals crashing loudly, furiously.
Perhaps the music one makes is loud and furious to drown
out one's own complaint. Perhaps the wildness expresses
something crazed. Or perhaps, in a rare moment of grace,
one might play the music without fury, in touch with

happiness, miraculously connected to God with praise in one's heart, *lamrot hakol*: Despite everything.

BREATH

HalleluYah: Praise God! The most breathy name of God is used here: *Yah*. Praise the Creator who breathed the breath of life into Adam and Eve and each one of us.

> "The rabbis, of blessed memory, said, 'Let every soul (*neshama*) praise God.' This means: Praise God with each and every breath (*neshima*), so you can say at every moment and continually, 'Blessed is the Merciful One, Ruler of the Universe, Master of this moment.'"
>
> *Or HaGanuz LaTzadikim*, p. 45

The last line in the final psalm of Rabbi Nachman's *tikkun* brings us to an awareness of the breath, rooting our being in the present moment, its reality and blessing. Fully present and mindful, we recognize that at all times, sick or well, we "have only moments to live" (Jon Kabat-Zinn, *Full Catastrophe Living*, 17).

A PRAYER FOR PRAYER

Rabbi Sheldon Zimmerman

O My God
My soul's companion
My heart's precious friend
I turn to You.

I need to close out the noise
To rise above the noise
The noise that interrupts—
The noise that separates—
The noise that isolates.
I need to hear You again.

In the silence of my innermost being,
In the fragments of my yearned-for wholeness,
I hear whispers of Your presence—
Echoes of the past when You were with me
When I felt Your nearness
When together we walked—
When You held me close, embraced me in Your love,
laughed with me in my joy.
I yearn to hear You again.

In your oneness, I find healing.
In the promise of Your love, I am soothed.
In Your wholeness, I too can become whole again.

Please listen to my call—
      help me find the words
      help me find the strength within
      help me shape my mouth, my voice, my heart
so that I can direct my spirit and find You in prayer
In words only my heart can speak
In songs only my soul can sing
Lifting my eyes and heart to You.

Adonai S'fatai Tiftach—open my lips, precious God,
so that I can speak with You again.

NOTES TO INTRODUCTION

1. Slight variations exist between the names given for these ten kinds of song in the Talmud, the *Zohar*, and in Rashi. Here is an integrated version of the ten types of songs, and the *sefirot* to which they correspond:

TYPE OF SONGS		CORRESPONDING *SEFIR*	
Ashrei	"Happy..."	*Keter*	"Crown"
Shir	"Song"	*Hokhmah*	"Wisdom"
Brakhah	"Blessing"	*Binah*	"Understanding"
Niggun	"Melody"	*Hessed*	"Lovingkindness"
Zemer	"Chant"	*G'vurah*	"Might"
Hallelu	"Praise/exhoration"	*Tiferet*	"Honor"
Lamenatzeah	"Songleader"	*Netzah*	"Glory"
Hodu	"Give thanks"	*Hod*	"Splendor"
Rinah	"Joy"	*Yesod*	"Secret"
Tehillah	"Praise"	*Malkhut*	"Majesty"

2. See *Rabbi Nachman's Tikkun: The Comprehensive Remedy*, compiled and translated by Avraham Greenbaum (Jerusalem/New York: Breslov Research Institute, 1984), Chapter 6, "Song," page 65.

3. The English word "sin" is problematic in its implications. The Hebrew word that is usually translated as "sin," "*ChaTA*," actually comes from a root that means "missing the target," which, alas, human beings do very often.

"Confession" in the Jewish sense means owning up and feeling regret for "missing the mark," and thereby being distant from God. Confession of sin should be viewed as a challenge, an opportunity for honest self-scrutiny, leading to catharsis, cleansing, and active reconciliation.

4. From *Tzava'at HaRIBASH* (p. 24; The Ethical Will of the Baal Shem Tov) and *Derekh Tzaddikim* (*Mikvah* 5: an anthology of the writings of leading Hasidic Masters). Special thanks to Chaim Kramer of the Breslov Research Institute for contributing this verse and its sources.

ABOUT THE CONTRIBUTORS AND THEIR BACKGROUNDS

Rabbi Eugene B. Borowitz (Reform) is the Sigmund L. Falk Distinguished Professor of Education and Jewish Religious Thought at Hebrew Union College-Jewish Institute of Religion in New York City, where he was ordained. His most recent book is *Renewing the Covenant: A Theology for the Postmodern Jew.*

Rabbi Rachel Cowan (Reform) directs the Jewish Life Program of the Nathan Cummings Foundation in New York City. Ordained by Hebrew Union College-Jewish Institute of Religion, she teaches and lectures extensively. Her own attachment to psalms as a resource for healing grows from her experience with her late husband Paul Cowan's struggle to find hope in the face of a fatal illness.

Rabbi Amy Eilberg (Conservative) is Director of Kol Haneshama, the Jewish hospice program of the Jewish Healing Center in the San Francisco Bay area. She was the first woman ordained by The Jewish Theological Seminary of America, in 1985.

Rabbi Nancy Flam (Reform) was ordained by the Hebrew Union College-Jewish Institute of Religion in 1989. For the past three years, she has served as West Coast Director of the Jewish Healing Center, based in San Francisco.

Rabbi Irving Greenberg (Orthodox) is the President and Cofounder of CLAL: National Jewish Center for Learning and Leadership, based in New York City. He is the author of *The Jewish Way*, a comprehensive and inspiring presentation of Judaism as revealed through its holy days.

Rabbi Maurice Lamm (Orthodox) received his ordination, B.A., M.A. and Honorary Doctorate from Yeshiva University, where he occupies a Chair in Rabbinics. He is President of the National Institute for Jewish Hospice, former Rabbi of Beth Jacob Congregation in Beverly Hills, California, and author of *The Jewish Way in Death and Mourning, Love and Marriage, Becoming a Jew,* and *Living Torah in America.*

Rabbi Harold M. Schulweis (Conservative) is spiritual leader of Valley Beth Shalom in Encino, California. Ordained at The Jewish Theological Seminary of America, he is Founding Chairman of the Jewish Foundation for Christian Rescuers, and author of the forthcoming book *For Those Who Can't Believe.*

Rabbi Charles Sheer (Orthodox) was ordained by Yeshiva University where he received an M.A. in Talmudic Literature. He enjoys teaching, counseling, and program work with his students at Columbia University, where he is the Jewish Chaplain.

Rabbi Harlan J. Wechsler (Conservative) is Rabbi of Congregation Or Zarua in New York City and the author of *What's So Bad About Guilt?* and the forthcoming *Old is Good.* He is Assistant Professor of Philosophy at The Jewish Theological Seminary of America, where he received his rabbinic ordination.

Rabbi Sheila Peltz Weinberg (Reconstructionist) is a graduate of the Reconstructionist Rabbinical College, and Rabbi of the Jewish Community of Amherst, Massachusetts, an unaffiliated liberal synagogue.

Rabbi Simkha Y. Weintraub, CSW (Conservative) serves as Program Consultant to the Jewish Healing Center. Ordained at The Jewish Theological Seminary of America, he is Director of Public Affairs for the New Israel Fund and maintains a private practice in Couples and Family Therapy in New York City.

Rabbi Sheldon Zimmerman (Reform), a graduate of Hebrew Union College-Jewish Institute of Religion, is Rabbi of Temple Emanu-El in Dallas, Texas, and the President of the Central Conference of American Rabbis.

SOME SUGGESTED READING AND RESOURCES

All publications listed below are in English.

FOR FURTHER EXPLORATION OF PSALMS:

The Book of Psalms: A New Translation According to the Traditional Hebrew Text. Philadelphia: Jewish Publication Society of America, 1972.

Davis, Rabbi Avrohom. *The Metsudah Tehillim: A New Linear Tehillim.* Translation and notes by Rabbi Avrohom Davis. New York: Metsudah Publications, 1983.

Feuer, Rabbi Avrohom Chaim. *Tehillim/Psalms: A New Translation with a Commentary anthologized from Talmudic, Midrashic, and Rabbinic Sources.* Commentary and overview by Rabbi Avrohom Chaim Feuer. 5 vols. New York: Mesorah Publications, 1977.

Hirsch, Rabbi Samson Raphael. *The Psalms.* Translation and Commentary by Rabbi Samson Raphael Hirsch. Jerusalem/New York: Feldheim Publishers, 1978.

Mitchell, Stephen. *A Book of Psalms: Selected and Adapted from the Hebrew.* New York: HarperCollins, 1993.

Rosenberg, Rabbi A.J. *The Book of Psalms: A New English Translation*. Translation of text, Rashi, and commentary by Rabbi A.J. Rosenberg. 3 vols. New York: The Judaica Press, 1991.

Weiser, Artur. *The Psalms: A Commentary*. Translated from the German by Herbert Hartwell. Philadelphia: Westminster Press, 1962.

FOR FURTHER EXPLORATION OF THE LIFE, STORIES, AND TEACHINGS OF RABBI NACHMAN OF BRESLOV:

Band, Arnold J. *Nahman of Bratslav: The Tales*. Translation, introduction, and commentaries by Arnold J. Band; preface by Joseph Dan. New York: Paulist Press, 1978.

Buber, Martin. *The Tales of Rabbi Nachman*. Translated from the German by Maurice Friedman. Atlantic Highlands, N.J.: Humanities Press International, 1989.

Green, Arthur. *Tormented Master: The Life and Spiritual Quest of Rabbi Nahman of Bratslav*. Woodstock, Vt.: Jewish Lights, 1993 (reissue).

Greenbaum, Avraham. *Rabbi Nachman's Tikkun: The Comprehensive Remedy*. Compiled and translated by Avraham Greenbaum. Jerusalem/New York: Breslov Research Institute, 1984.

Kaplan, Aryeh. *Rabbi Nachman's Wisdom by Rabbi* Nathan of *Nemirov*. Translated and annotated by Rabbi Aryeh Kaplan; edited by Rabbi Aryeh Rosenfeld. Brooklyn, N.Y.: Gross Brothers, 1973.

Mykoff, Moshe and the Breslov Research Institute. *The Empty Chair: Finding Hope & Joy—Timeless Wisdom* from *a Hasidic Master, Rebbe Nachman of Breslov*. Woodstock, Vt: Jewish Lights, 1994.

Mykoff, Moshe. *Likutey Moharan: Collected Teachings of Rebbe Nachman of Breslov*. Translated and edited by Moshe Mykoff and Ozer Bergman; annotated by Chaim Kramer. 4 vols. Jerusalem/New York: Breslov Research Institute, 1993.

Schwartz, Howard. *The Captive Soul of the Messiah: New Tales about Reb Nachman.* Illustrated by Mark Podwal. New York: Schocken Books, 1983.

Shulman, Y. David. *The Chambers of the Palace: Teachings* of *Rabbi Nachman of Bratslav.* Northvale, N.J.: Jason Aronson, 1993.

Steinsaltz, Adin. *Beggars and Prayers: Adin Steinsaltz Retells the Tales of Rabbi Nachman of Bratslav.* Edited by Jonathan Omer-Man. New York: Basic Books, 1979.

For additional publications by and about Rabbi Nachman, contact the Breslov Research Institute:

BRESLOV RESEARCH INSTITUTE
P. O. Box 587
Monsey, NY 10952-0587
Tel: (914) 425-4258
Fax: (914) 425-3018

BRESLOV RESEARCH INSTITUTE
P. O. Box 5370
Jerusalem, Israel 91053
Tel: (011-972-2) 824-641
Fax: (011-972-2) 825-542

OTHER RESOURCES RELATED TO JEWISH SPIRITUAL HEALING IN TIMES OF ILLNESS:

Gates of Healing. Central Conference of American Rabbis, 1988.

The Outstretched Arm (newsletter). San Francisco, Calif.: Jewish Healing Center.

Refuah Shelemah: Fountain of Life. Rabbinical Assembly, 1975 (available through K'tav Publications, Hoboken, N.J.).

Schur, Rabbi Tsvi G. *Illness and Crisis: Coping the Jewish Way.* New York: National Conference of Synagogue Youth, 1987.

When the Body Hurts, the Soul Still Longs to Sing. San Francisco, Calif.: Jewish Healing Center, 1992.

With Healing on Its Wings: Contemplations in Times of Illness. London, England: Masorti Publications, 1992.

Yurow, Jane Handler and Kim Hetherington. *Give Me Your Hand: Traditional and Practical Guidance on Visiting the Sick.* Washington, D.C.: Adas Israel Congregation, 1988.

HELPFUL ORGANIZATIONS

Many national and community-based agencies offer programs and publications to help those confronting illness—their own or that of a loved one.

Here are some valuable resources.

THE JEWISH HEALING CENTER

141 Alton Avenue
San Francisco, CA 94116
Tel: (415) 387-4999
Fax: (415) 661-9403
See page 117.

JACS—JEWISH ALCOHOLICS, CHEMICALLY DEPENDENT
PERSONS, AND SIGNIFICANT OTHERS

426 West 58th Street
New York, NY 10019
Tel: (212) 397-4197
Fax: (212) 489-6229
JACS is a supplement to 12-step programs, providing Jewish alcholics, addicts, and family members with

opportunities for connection to other Jews who previously had no outlet for sharing the reality of being Jewish and affected by addiction.

COORDINATING COUNCIL ON BIKUR CHOLIM (CCBC)

130 East 59th Street, Room 306
New York, NY 10022
Tel: (212) 836-1197
Fax: (212) 836-1372

The CCBC can provide names and phone numbers of people worldwide who help by observing the *mitzvah/ commandment* of *bikur cholim*, attending to the needs of those who are ill. It trains *bikur cholim* volunteers in the greater New York area.

NATIONAL INSTITUTE FOR JEWISH HOSPICE (NIJH)

8723 Alden Drive, Suite 652
Los Angeles, CA 90048
Tel: (310) 854-3036

Established in 1985 to help alleviate suffering in serious and terminal illness, the NIJH offers a range of publications (dealing with issues such as understanding pain, how to console, the orphaned adult, and truth-telling) and hotline counselling (1-800-446-4448), maintains a national data base for Jewish resources, and sponsors research. Special NIJH materials offer a Jewish approach to timely subjects such as euthanasia and physician-assisted death.

OTHER RESOURCES

Local synagogues, Jewish Community Centers, and YM-YWHA's, many of which are integrating support groups, workshops, and healing services into their ongoing program.

Jewish Family Service agencies (contact your local Federation of Jewish Philanthropies for name, address, and phone number), which offer individual counselling, support groups, educational seminars, and referral services.

Local chapters of national organizations dedicated to helping those with particular diseases, as well as their family and friends—such as Cancer Care, Alzheimers Association, the Leukemia Society of America, American Heart Association, and so on. Many of these sponsor workshops and support groups, have helpful printed information, and can even help over the phone (such as the Cancer Information Line—1-800-4-CANCER).

ABOUT THE JEWISH HEALING CENTER

THE JEWISH HEALING CENTER IS A NOT-FOR-PROFIT SERVICE, education, and resource organization dedicated to meeting the spiritual needs of Jews living with chronic or acute illness.

It offers healing prayer services, spiritual support groups, educational workshops and seminars, pastoral counseling, a library, and information and referral services, reaching out to Jews who are ill and their loved ones, to rabbis and chaplains, and to health care professionals.

For more information about programs and resources, or to make a contribution, please contact:

Rabbi Nancy Flam, West Coast Director
The Jewish Healing Center
141 Alton Avenue
San Francisco, CA 94116
Tel: (415) 387-4999
Fax: (415) 661-9403

About JEWISH LIGHTS Publishing

People of all faiths and backgrounds yearn for books that attract, engage, educate and spiritually inspire.

Our principal goal is to stimulate thought and help all people learn about who the Jewish People are, where they come from, and what the future can be made to hold. While people of our diverse Jewish heritage are the primary audience, our books speak to the Christian world as well and will broaden their understanding of Judaism and the roots of their own faith.

We bring to you authors who are at the forefront of spiritual thought and experience. While each has something different to say, they all say it in a voice that you can hear.

Our books are designed to welcome you and then to engage, stimulate and inspire. We judge our success not only by whether or not our books are beautiful and commercially successful, but by whether or not they make a difference in your life.

We at Jewish Lights take great care to produce beautiful books that present meaningful spiritual content in a form that reflects the art of making high quality books. Therefore, we want to acknowledge those who contributed to the production of this book.

PRODUCTION
Wendy Kilborn

EDITORIAL & PROOFREADING
Sandra Korinchak

BOOK & COVER DESIGN
Karen Savary, Deering, New Hampshire

TYPE
Set in Book Antiqua & Albertus
Karen Savary, Deering, New Hampshire

HEBREW
Tali Dowek, Tel Aviv, Israel

COVER PRINTING
Phoenix Color, Long Island City, New York

PRINTING AND BINDING
Book Press, Brattleboro, Vermont

Spiritual Inspiration for Family Life

MOURNING & MITZVAH
A Guided Journal for Walking the Mourner's Path
Through Grief to Healing • WITH OVER 60 GUIDED EXERCISES •
by *Anne Brener, L.C.S.W.*

"Fully engaging in mourning means you will be a different person than before you began."

For those who mourn a death, for those who would help them, for those who face a loss of any kind, Anne Brener teaches us the power and strength available to us in the fully experienced mourning process. Guided writing exercises help stimulate the processes of both conscious and unconscious healing.

"A stunning book! It offers an exploration in depth of the place where psychology and religious ritual intersect, and the name of that place is Truth."
—Rabbi Harold Kushner, *author of* When Bad Things Happen to Good People

"This book is marvelous. It is a work that I wish I had written. It is the best book on this subject that I have ever seen." —*Rabbi Levi Meier, Ph.D., Chaplain, Cedars Sinai Medical Center, Los Angeles, Orthodox Rabbi, Clinical Psychologist*

7 1/2" x 9", 288 pp. Quality Paperback Original, ISBN 1-879045-23-0 **$19.95**

THE PREMIERE BOOK IN A LANDMARK NEW THREE-VOLUME SERIES

LIFECYCLES
Jewish Women on Life Passages
& Personal Milestones
Edited and with introductions by *Rabbi Debra Orenstein*

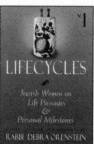

In self-aware, passionate, and insightful voices, 50 leading thinkers come together to explore tradition and innovation in personal ritual and spirituality. Speaking to women of all backgrounds, it covers the entire spectrum of life's passages, from ceremonies around childbirth to new perspectives on aging. Other topics include marriage, singlehood, conversion, coming out, parenting, divorce, and mid-life.

6" x 9", 480 pp. Hardcover, ISBN 1-879045-14-1 **$24.95**

HEALING OF SOUL, HEALING OF BODY:
Spiritual Leaders Unfold the Strength and Solace in Psalms
Edited by *Rabbi Simkha Y. Weintraub, CSW*

A source of solace for those who are facing illness, as well as those who care for them. The ten Psalms which form the core of this healing resource were originally selected 200 years ago by Rabbi Nachman of Breslov as a "complete remedy." Today, for anyone coping with illness, they continue to provide a wellspring of strength.

Each Psalm is newly translated, making it clear and accessible, and each one is introduced by an eminent rabbi, men and women reflecting different movements and backgrounds. To all who are living with the pain and uncertainty of illness, this spiritual resource offers an anchor of spiritual comfort.

6" x 9", 128 pp. (est.) illus., 2-color text. Quality Paperback Original, ISBN 1-879045-31-1 **$13.95**

Spiritual Inspiration for Family Life

IN GOD'S NAME

For children K-5

by *Sandy Sasso*

Full color illustrations by *Phoebe Stone*

Like an ancient myth in its poetic text and vibrant illustrations, this modern fable about the search for God's name celebrates the diversity and, at the same time, the unity of all the people of the world. Each seeker claims he or she alone knows the answer. Finally, they come together and learn what God's name really is, sharing the ultimate harmony of belief in one God by people of all faiths, all backgrounds.

Illus. by Phoebe Stone

"I got goosebumps when I read *In God's Name*, its language and illustrations are that moving. This is a book children will love and the whole family will cherish for its beauty and power."
—*Francine Klagsbrun*, author of *Mixed Feelings: Love, Hate, Rivalry, and Reconciliation Among Brothers and Sisters*

9" x 12", 32 pp. Hardcover, Full color illus., ISBN 1-879045-26-5 **$16.95**

For Children

GOD'S PAINTBRUSH

by *Sandy Eisenberg Sasso*

Full color illustrations by *Annette Compton*

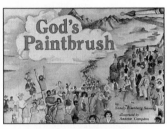

MULTICULTURAL, NON-SECTARIAN, NON-DENOMINATIONAL. Invites children of all faiths and backgrounds to encounter God openly in their own lives. Wonderfully interactive, provides questions adult and child can explore together at the end of each episode.

"The most exciting religious children's book I have seen in years."
—*Sylvia Avner, Children's Librarian, 92nd St. "Y," NYC*

"An excellent way to honor the imaginative breadth and depth of the spiritual life of the young." —*Dr. Robert Coles, Harvard University*

• AWARD WINNER •

For children K–4 elementary

11"x 8½", 32 pp. Hardcover, Full color illustrations, ISBN 1-879045-22-2 **$15.95**

THE *NEW* JEWISH BABY BOOK

Names, Ceremonies, Customs — A Guide for Today's Families

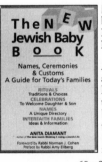

by *Anita Diamant*

Foreword by *Rabbi Norman J. Cohen, Dean, HUC–JIR, NYC*

Introduction by *Rabbi Amy Eilberg*

A complete guide to the customs and rituals for welcoming a new child to the world and into the Jewish community, and for commemorating this joyous event in family life–whatever your family constellation. Updated, revised and expanded edition of the highly acclaimed *The Jewish Baby Book*. Includes new ceremonies for girls, celebrations in interfaith families. Also contains a unique directory of names that reflects the rich diversity of the Jewish experience.

"A book that all Jewish parents—no matter how religious—will find fascinating as well as useful. It is a perfect shower or new baby gift." — *Pamela Abrams, Exec. Editor,* Parents Magazine

6"x 9", 328 pp. Quality Paperback Original, ISBN 1-879045-28-1 **$15.95**

PUTTING GOD ON THE GUEST LIST

AWARD WINNER

How to Reclaim the Spiritual Meaning of Your Child's Bar or Bat Mitzvah

"Best Religion Book of the Year"

by *Rabbi Jeffrey K. Salkin*

Foreword by *Rabbi Sandy Eisenberg Sasso*

Introduction by *Rabbi William H. Lebeau, Vice Chancellor, JTS*

Joining explanation, instruction and inspiration, helps parent and child truly *be there* when the moment of Sinai is recreated in their lives. Asks and answers such fundamental questions as how did Bar and Bat Mitzvah originate? What is the lasting significance of the event? How to make the event more spiritually meaningful?

"Shows the way to restore spirituality and depth to every young Jew's most important rite of passage." — *Rabbi Joseph Telushkin, author of* Jewish Literacy

"I hope every family planning a Bar Mitzvah celebration reads Rabbi Salkin's book."
— *Rabbi Harold S. Kushner, author of* When Bad Things Happen to Good People

6"x 9", 184 pp. Quality Paperback, ISBN 1-879045-10-9 **$14.95** HC, ISBN -20-6 **$21.95**

Add Greater Understanding to Your Life

JEWISH LIGHTS Classic Reprints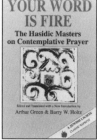

TORMENTED MASTER
The Life and Spiritual Quest of Rabbi Nahman of Bratslav
by *Arthur Green*

Explores the personality and religious quest of Nahman of Bratslav (1772–1810), one of Hasidism's major figures. It unlocks the great themes of spiritual searching that make him a figure of universal religious importance.

"A model of clarity and percipience....Utterly relevant to our time."
                                        —*New York Times Book Review*
                6"x 9", 408 pp. Quality Paperback, ISBN 1-879045-11-7 **$17.95**

THE LAST TRIAL
On the Legends and Lore of the Command to Abraham to Offer Isaac as a Sacrifice
by *Shalom Spiegel*

New Introduction by *Judah Goldin, Emeritus Professor, University of Pennsylvania*

A classic. An eminent Jewish scholar examines the total body of texts, legends, and traditions referring to the Binding of Isaac and weaves them all together into a definitive study of the *Akedah* as one of the central events in all of human history.
"A model in the history of biblical interpretation, and a centerpiece for Jewish-Christian discussion."—*Dr. Michael Fishbane, Nathan Cummings Professor of Jewish Studies, University of Chicago*

                6"x 9", 208 pp. Quality Paperback, ISBN 1-879045-29-X **$17.95**

ASPECTS OF RABBINIC THEOLOGY
by *Solomon Schechter*

Including the original Preface from the 1909 edition
& *Louis Finkelstein's* Introduction to the 1961 edition
with an important new Introduction by *Dr. Neil Gillman, Chair, Department of Jewish Philosophy, The Jewish Theological Seminary of America*

Learned yet highly accessible classic statement of the ideas that form the religious consciousness of the Jewish people at large, by one of the great minds of Jewish scholarship of our century.
"This is the only book on the theology of Judaism written 100 years ago that anyone can read today with profit." — *Jacob Neusner, Distinguished Research Professor of Religious Studies, University of South Florida*

"A better antidote could not be found for the still too prevalent Christian ignorance of the richness and depth of the Jewish heritage." — *The Rev. Dr. Paul M. van Buren, Honorarprofessor Of Systematic Theology, Heidelberg University*

                6" x 9", 440 pp. Quality Paperback, ISBN 1-879045-24-9 **$18.95**

YOUR WORD IS FIRE
The Hasidic Masters on Contemplative Prayer
Edited and translated by *Arthur Green* and *Barry W. Holtz*

The power of prayer for spiritual renewal and personal transformation is at the core of all religious traditions. From the teachings of the Hasidic Masters the editors have gleaned "hints as to the various rungs of inner prayer and how they are attained." These parables and aphorisms of the Hasidic masters pierce to the heart of the modern reader's search for God.

"Opens up some of the more accessible realms of the Jewish inner life."
                                        — *Eugene B. Borowitz,* Sh'ma
                6"x 9", 152 pp. Quality Paperback, ISBN 1-879045-25-7 **$14.95**

Add Greater Meaning to Your Life

FAITH AFTER THE HOLOCAUST?

AWARD WINNER **THE SPIRIT OF RENEWAL**

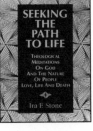

NEW!
in paperback

Finding Faith After the Holocaust
by *Edward Feld*

"Boldly redefines the landscape of Jewish religious thought after the Holocaust." — *Rabbi Lawrence Kushner*

Trying to understand the Holocaust and addressing the question of faith after the Holocaust, Rabbi Feld explores three key cycles of destruction and recovery in Jewish history, each of which radically reshaped Jewish understanding of God, people, and the world.

"Undoubtedly the most moving book I have read....'Must' reading."
— *Rabbi Howard A. Addison*, Conservative Judaism

"A profound meditation on Jewish history [and the Holocaust]....Christians, as well as many others, need to share in this story." —*The Rt. Rev. Frederick H. Borsch, Ph.D., Episcopal Bishop of L.A.*

6"x 9", 216 pp. Hardcover, ISBN 1-879045-06-0 **$22.95**
6"x 9", 224 pp. Quality Paperback, ISBN 1-879045-40-0 **$16.95**

SEEKING THE PATH TO LIFE AWARD WINNER

Theological Meditations On God
and the Nature of People, Love, Life and Death
by *Rabbi Ira F. Stone,*
Ornamentation by *Annie Stone*

For people who never thought they would read a book of theology—let alone understand it, enjoy it, savor it and have it affect the way they think about their lives.

In 45 intense meditations, each a page or two in length, Stone takes us on explorations of the most basic human struggles: life and death, love and anger, peace and war, covenant and exile.

"Exhilarating—unlike any other reading that I have done in years."
—*Rabbi Neil Gillman, The Jewish Theological Seminary*
"A bold book....The reader of any faith will be inspired, challenged and led more deeply into their own encounter with God."
— *The Rev. Carla Berkedal, Episcopal Priest, Executive Director of Earth Ministry*

6"x 9", 144 pp. Hardcover, ISBN 1-879045-17-6 **$19.95**

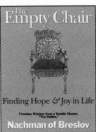

THE EMPTY CHAIR: FINDING HOPE & JOY
Timeless Wisdom from a Hasidic Master, Rebbe Nachman of Breslov
Adapted by *Moshe Mykoff* and *the Breslov Research Institute*

A "little treasure" of aphorisms and advice for living joyously and spiritually today, written 200 years ago, but startlingly fresh in meaning and use. Challenges and helps us to move from stress and sadness to hope and joy.

Teacher, guide and spiritual master—Rebbe Nachman provides vital words of inspiration and wisdom for life today for people of any faith, or of no faith.

4" x 6", 128 pp. Hardcover, ISBN 1-879045-16-8 **$9.95**

Motivation & Inspiration for Recovery

TWELVE JEWISH STEPS TO RECOVERY
A Personal Guide To Turning From Alcoholism & Other Addictions...Drugs, Food, Gambling, Sex

by *Rabbi Kerry M. Olitzky* & *Stuart A. Copans*, M.D.
Preface by Abraham J. Twerski, M.D.
Introduction by Rabbi Sheldon Zimmerman
Illustrations by Maty Grünberg
"Getting Help" by JACS Foundation

A Jewish perspective on the Twelve Steps of addiction recovery programs with consolation, inspiration and motivation for recovery. It draws from traditional sources, and quotes from what recovering Jewish people say about their experiences with addictions of all kinds. Inspiring illustrations of the twelve gates of the Old City of Jerusalem.

Experts Praise *Twelve Jewish Steps To Recovery*

"Recommended reading for people of all denominations." — Rabbi Abraham J. Twerski, M.D.

"I read Twelve Jewish Steps with the eyes of a Christian and came away renewed in my heart. I felt like I had visited my Jewish roots. These authors have deep knowledge of recovery as viewed by Alcoholics Anonymous." — Rock J. Stack, M.A., L.L.D. Manager of Clinical/Pastoral Education, Hazelden Foundation

"This book is the first aimed directly at helping the addicted person and family. Everyone affected or interested should read it." — Sheila B. Blume, M.D., C.A.C., Medical Director, Alcoholism, Chemical Dependency and Compulsive Gambling Programs, South Oaks Hospital, Amityville, NY

Readers Praise *Twelve Jewish Steps To Recovery*

"A God-send. Literally. A book from the higher power." — New York, NY

"Looking forward to using it in my practice." —Michigan City, IN

"Made me feel as though 12 Steps were for me, too." — Long Beach, CA

"Excellent–changed my life." — Elkhart Lake, WI

6" x 9", 136 pp. Quality Paperback, ISBN 1-879045-09-5 **$12.95**

RECOVERY FROM *Codependence*
A Jewish Twelve Steps Guide to Healing Your Soul

by *Rabbi Kerry M. Olitzky*
Foreword by *Marc Galanter, M.D., Director,*
Division of Alcoholism & Drug Abuse, NYU Medical Center
Afterword by *Harriet Rossetto, Director, Gateways Beit T'shuvah*

For the estimated 90% of America struggling with the addiction of a family member or loved one, or involved in a dysfunctional family or relationship. A follow-up to the ground-breaking *Twelve Jewish Steps to Recovery*.

"The disease of chemical dependency is also a family illness. Rabbi Olitzky offers spiritual hope and support." —*Jerry Spicer, President, Hazelden*

"Another major step forward in finding the sources and resources of healing, both physical and spiritual, in our tradition." —*Rabbi Sheldon Zimmerman, Temple Emanu-El, Dallas, TX*

6" x 9", 160 pp. Hardcover, ISBN 1-879045-27-3 **$21.95**
6" x 9", 160 pp. Quality Paperback, ISBN 1-879045-32-X **$13.95**

Motivation & Inspiration for Recovery

RENEWED EACH DAY
Daily Twelve Step Recovery Meditations
Based on the Bible
by *Rabbi Kerry M. Olitzky* & *Aaron Z.*

VOLUME I: Genesis & Exodus
Introduction by *Rabbi Michael A. Signer*
Afterword by JACS Foundation

VOLUME II: Leviticus, Numbers & Deuteronomy
Introduction by *Sharon M. Strassfeld*
Afterword by *Rabbi Harold M. Schulweis*

Using a seven day/weekly guide format, a recovering person and a spiritual leader who is reaching out to addicted people reflect on the traditional weekly Bible reading. They bring strong spiritual support for daily living and recovery from addictions of all kinds: alcohol, drugs, eating, gambling and sex. A profound sense of the religious spirit soars through their words and brings all people in Twelve Step recovery programs home to a rich and spiritually enlightening tradition.

"Meets a vital need; it offers a chance for people turning from alcoholism and addiction to renew their spirits and draw upon the Jewish tradition to guide and enrich their lives."
—*Rabbi Irving (Yitz) Greenberg, President, CLAL,*
The National Jewish Center for Learning and Leadership

"Will benefit anyone familiar with a 'religion of the Book.' Jews, Christians, Muslims. . . ."
—*Ernest Kurtz, author of* Not-God: A History of Alcoholics
Anonymous & The Spirituality of Imperfection

"An enduring impact upon the faith community as it seeks to blend the wisdom of the ages represented in the tradition with the twelve steps to recovery and wholeness."
—*Robert H. Albers, Ph.D., Editor,* Journal of Ministry in Addiction & Recovery

Beautiful Two-Volume Set.
6"x 9", V. I, 224 pp. / V. II, 280 pp., Quality Paperback, ISBN 1-879045-21-4   **$27.90**

ONE HUNDRED BLESSINGS EVERY DAY
Daily Twelve Step Recovery Affirmations, Exercises for Personal Growth & Renewal Reflecting Seasons of the Jewish Year
by *Dr. Kerry M. Olitzky*
with selected meditations prepared by *Rabbi James Stone Goodman, Danny Siegel,* and *Rabbi Gordon Tucker*
Foreword by *Rabbi Neil Gillman,*
The Jewish Theological Seminary of America
Afterword by *Dr. Jay Holder, Director, Exodus Treatment Center*

Recovery is a conscious choice from moment to moment, day in and day out. In this helpful and healing book of daily recovery meditations, Kerry Olitzky gives us words to live by day after day, throughout the annual cycle of holiday observances and special Sabbaths of the Jewish calendar.

For those facing the struggles of daily living, *One Hundred Blessings Every Day* brings solace and hope to anyone who is open to healing and to the recovery-oriented teachings that can be gleaned from the Bible and Jewish tradition.

4½" x 6½", Quality Paperback, 432 pp. ISBN 1-879045-30-3   **$14.95**

Spiritual Inspiration for Daily Living . . .

THE BOOK OF WORDS
Talking Spiritual Life, Living Spiritual Talk
by *Lawrence Kushner*

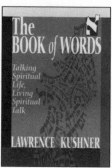

In the incomparable manner of his extraordinary *The Book of Letters: A Mystical Hebrew Alphabet,* Kushner now lifts up and shakes the dust off primary religious words we use to describe the spiritual dimension of life. The *Words* take on renewed spiritual significance, adding power and focus to the lives we live every day.

For each word Kushner offers us a startling, moving and insightful explication, and pointed readings from classical Jewish sources that further illuminate the concept. He concludes with a short exercise that helps unite the spirit of the word with our actions in the world.

6" x 9", 152 pp. Hardcover, two-color text ISBN 1-879045-35-4 **$21.95**

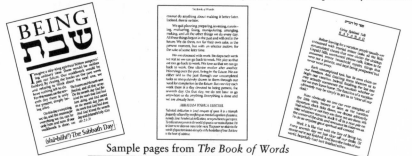

Sample pages from *The Book of Words*

AWARD WINNER
THE BOOK OF LETTERS
A Mystical Hebrew Alphabet
by *Rabbi Lawrence Kushner*

In calligraphy by the author. Folktales about and exploration of the mystical meanings of the Hebrew Alphabet. Open the old prayerbook-like pages of *The Book of Letters* and you will enter a special world of sacred tradition and religious feeling. More than just symbols, all twenty-two letters of the Hebrew alphabet overflow with meanings and personalities of their own.

Rabbi Kushner draws from ancient Judaic sources, weaving Talmudic commentary, Hasidic folktales, and Kabbalistic mysteries around the letters.

"A book which is in love with Jewish letters." — Isaac Bashevis Singer

• **Popular Hardcover Edition**
6" x 9", 80 pp. Hardcover, two colors, inspiring new Foreword.
ISBN 1-879045-00-1 **$24.95**

• **Deluxe Gift Edition**
9" x 12", 80 pp. Hardcover, four-color text, ornamentation, in a beautiful slipcase.
ISBN 1-879045-01-X **$79.95**

• **Collector's Limited Edition**
9" x 12", 80 pp. Hardcover, gold embossed pages, hand assembled slipcase. With silkscreened print.

Limited to 500 signed and numbered copies.

ISBN 1-879045-04-4 **$349.00**

To see a sample page at no obligation, call us

. . . .The Kushner Series

GOD WAS IN THIS PLACE & I, i
DID NOT KNOW
Finding Self, Spirituality & Ultimate Meaning
by *Lawrence Kushner*

Who am I? Who is God? Kushner creates inspiring interpretations of Jacob's dream in Genesis, opening a window into Jewish spirituality for people of all faiths and backgrounds.

In a fascinating blend of scholarship, imagination, psychology and history, seven Jewish spiritual masters ask and answer fundamental questions of human experience.

"A brilliant fabric of classic rabbinic interpretations, Hasidic insights and literary criticism which warms us and sustains us."
— *Dr. Norman J. Cohen, Dean, Hebrew Union College, NY*

"Rich and intriguing." —*M. Scott Peck, M.D., author of* The Road Less Traveled

6"x 9", 192 pp. Hardcover, ISBN 1-879045-05-2 **$21.95**

6"x 9", 192 pp. Quality Paperback, ISBN 1-879045-33-8 **$16.95**

HONEY FROM THE ROCK
An Introduction to Jewish Mysticism
by *Lawrence Kushner*

An introduction to the ten gates of Jewish mysticism and how it applies to daily life.

"Quite simply the easiest introduction to Jewish mysticism you can read."

"Honey from the Rock captures the flavor and spark of Jewish mysticism. . . . Read it and be rewarded." —*Elie Wiesel*

"A work of love, lyrical beauty, and prophetic insight. "
—*Father Malcolm Boyd,* The Christian Century

6"x 9", 168 pp. Quality Paperback, ISBN 1-879045-02-8 **$14.95**

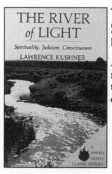

THE RIVER OF LIGHT
Spirituality, Judaism, Consciousness
by *Lawrence Kushner*

A "manual" for all spiritual travelers who would attempt a spiritual journey in our times. Taking us step by step, Kushner allows us to discover the meaning of our own quest: "to allow the river of light—the deepest currents of consciousness—to rise to the surface and animate our lives."

"Philosophy and mystical fantasy...exhilarating speculative flights launched from the Bible....Anybody—Jewish, Christian, or otherwise...will find this book an intriguing experience."—The Kirkus Reviews

"A very important book."—*Rabbi Adin Steinsaltz*

6"x 9", 180 pp. Quality Paperback, ISBN 1-879045-03-6 **$14.95**

Bring Spirituality into Your Daily Life

BEING GOD'S PARTNER
How to Find the Hidden Link Between Spirituality and Your Work
by *Dr. Jeffrey K. Salkin*
Introduction by *Norman Lear*

Being God's
Partner

*How to Find the
Hidden Link
Between Spirituality
and Your Work*

by Dr. Jeffrey K. Salkin
Introduction by Norman Lear

A book that will challenge people of every denomination to reconcile the cares of work and soul. A groundbreaking book about spirituality and the work world, from a Jewish perspective. Helps the reader find God in the ethical striving and search for meaning in the professions and in business. Critiques our modern culture of workaholism and careerism, and offers practical suggestions for balancing your professional life and spiritual self.

Being God's Partner will inspire people of all faiths and no faith to find greater meaning in their work, and see themselves doing God's work in the world.

"His is an eloquent voice, bearing an important and concrete message of authentic Jewish religion. The book is engaging, easy to read and hard to put down — and it will make a difference and change people."
— Jacob Neusner, Distinguished Research Professor of Religious Studies, University of South Florida, author of *The Doubleday Anchor Reference Library Introduction to Rabbinic Literature*

6" x 9", 175 pp. (est.) Hardcover, ISBN 1-879045-37-0 **$19.95**

Available: October '94

SELF, STRUGGLE & CHANGE
Family Conflict Stories in Genesis and their Insights for Our Lives
by *Dr. Norman J. Cohen*

SELF,
STRUGGLE
& CHANGE
Family Conflict
Stories in Genesis
and their Insights
for Our Lives
🐟
by Dr. Norman J. Cohen

How do I find greater wholeness in my life and in my family's life?

The stress of late-20th-century living only brings new variations to timeless personal struggles. The people described by the biblical writers of Genesis were in situations and relationships very much like our own. We identify with them. Their stories still speak to us because they are about the same problems we deal with every day.

A modern master of biblical interpretation brings us greater understanding of the ancient text and of ourselves in this intriguing re-telling of conflict between husband and wife, father and son, brothers, and sisters.

6" x 9", 200 pp. (est.) Hardcover, ISBN 1-879045-19-2 **$21.95** (est.)

Available: November '94

SO THAT YOUR VALUES LIVE ON
Ethical Wills & How To Prepare Them
Edited by *Rabbi Jack Riemer & Professor Nathaniel Stampfer*

So that
your values
live on
Ethical Wills
and how to
prepare them

A cherished Jewish tradition, ethical wills—parents writing to children or grandparents to grandchildren—sum up what people have learned and express what they want most for, and from, their loved ones. Includes an intensive guide, **"How to Write Your Own Ethical Will,"** and a topical index. A marvelous treasury of wills: Herzl, Sholom Aleichem, Israelis, Holocaust victims, contemporary American Jews.

"This remarkable volume will enrich all those who will read it and meditate upon its infinite wisdom." — *Elie Wiesel*

6"x 9", 272 pp. Quality Paperback, ISBN 1-879045-34-6 **$16.95** HC, ISBN -07-9 **$23.95**

Coming 1995

HOW TO BE A PERFECT STRANGER: An Ecumenical Guide to Religious Etiquette

by *Richard Siegel and William Shanken*

Explains the rituals and celebrations of America's major religions/denominations, helping an interested guest to feel comfortable, participate to the fullest extent feasible and avoid violating anyone's religious principles.

(HC) **$24.95** (est.)

LIFECYCLES 2: JEWISH WOMEN ON LIFE THEMES & CYCLES OF MEANING

Topics include identity, sexuality, spirituality, prayer, doing good, health, home, and friendship.

(HC) **$24.95** (est.)

GODWRESTLING: New Edition

by *Arthur Ocean Waskow*

Revised, Updated, Expanded 20th Anniversary Edition of this spiritual classic by one of the most creative minds in the Jewish renewal movement.

(HC) **$21.95** (est.)

Mystical Bookmark
22k Gold Electroplated Solid Brass

From

The Book of Letters: A Mystical Hebrew Alphabet

by Rabbi Lawrence Kushner
all in his own calligraphy

1¹/₄" x 1⁷/₈" $10.00

Why a four-pronged *shin*?

According to *Sefer HaTemunah*, one letter is missing from our present alphabet. It will only be revealed in the future. The author explains that every defect in our universe is mysteriously connected with this unimaginable consonant whose sound will create undreamed of words and worlds, transforming repression into Loving.

On the left side of the black leather Tefillin box worn on the forehead during morning prayers there is a four-pronged *shin*. Some suspect that this may be the missing Letter whose name and pronunciation must wait for another universe. Yet, nevertheless, every morning, we wear it right between our eyes.

Order Information

_____	Aspects of Rabbinic Theology (pb), $18.95	_____
_____	Being God's Partner (hc), $19.95 (est.) OCT. '94	_____
_____	The Empty Chair (hc), $ 9.95	_____
_____	God's Paintbrush (hc), $15.95	_____
_____	Healing of Soul, Healing of Body (pb), $13.95	_____
_____	In God's Name (hc), $16.95	_____
_____	The Last Trial (pb), $17.95	_____
_____	Lifecycles, Volume One (hc), $24.95	_____
_____	Mourning & Mitzvah (pb), $19.95	_____
_____	The NEW Jewish Baby Book (pb), $15.95	_____
_____	Putting God on the Guest List (hc), $21.95; (pb), $14.95	_____
_____	Seeking the Path to Life (hc), $19.95	_____
_____	Self, Struggle & Change (hc), $21.95 (est.) NOV. '94	_____
_____	So That Your Values Live On (hc), $23.95; (pb), $16.95	_____
_____	Spirit of Renewal (hc), $22.95; (pb), $16.95	_____
_____	Tormented Master (pb), $17.95	_____
_____	Your Word Is Fire (pb), $14.95	_____

• The Kushner Series •

The Book of Letters

_____	– Popular Hardcover Edition (hc), $24.95*	_____
_____	– Deluxe Presentation Edition(hc), $79.95, *plus* $5.95 s/h	_____
_____	– Collector's Limited Edition, $349.00, *plus* $12.95 s/h	_____
_____	The Book of Words (hc), $21.95*	_____
_____	God Was In This Place... (hc), $21.95; (pb) $16.95*	_____
_____	Honey from the Rock (pb), $14.95*	_____
_____	River of Light (pb), $14.95*	_____
_____	THE KUSHNER SERIES — 5 books *marked with asterisk above*, $93.75	_____

• Motivation & Inspiration for Recovery •

_____	One Hundred Blessings Every Day, (pb) $14.95 *	_____
_____	Recovery From Codependence, (hc) $21.95; (pb) $13.95*	_____
_____	Renewed Each Day, 2-Volume Set, (pb) $27.90*	_____
_____	Twelve Jewish Steps To Recovery, (hc) $19.95; (pb) $12.95*	_____
_____	**THE COMPLETE RECOVERY SET – 20% SAVINGS** **5 Books** *marked with asterisk above* **+ Print Portfolio** — **$99.75**	_____

For s/h, add $3.00 for the first book, $1.50 each additional book   _____

All set prices include shipping/handling   **Total** $ _____

Check enclosed for $ _____ *payable to:* JEWISH LIGHTS Publishing

Charge my credit card: ❏ MasterCard   ❏ Visa   ❏ Discover   ❏ AMEX

Credit Card # _____ Expires _____

Name on card _____

Signature _____ Phone (_____) _____

Name _____

Street _____

City / State / Zip _____

Phone, fax, or mail to: JEWISH LIGHTS Publishing
Box 237, Sunset Farm Offices, Route 4, Woodstock, Vermont 05091
Tel (802) 457-4000   *Fax* (802) 457-4004
Credit card orders (800) 962-4544 (9ᴀᴍ–5ᴘᴍ ET Monday–Friday)
Generous discounts on quantity orders. SATISFACTION GUARANTEED. Prices subject to change.
AVAILABLE FROM BETTER BOOKSTORES. TRY YOUR BOOKSTORE FIRST.